1 MONTH OF
FREE
READING

at
www.ForgottenBooks.com

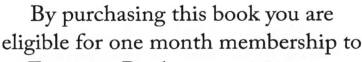

By purchasing this book you are eligible for one month membership to ForgottenBooks.com, giving you unlimited access to our entire collection of over 1,000,000 titles via our web site and mobile apps.

To claim your free month visit:

www.forgottenbooks.com/free905695

ISBN 978-0-266-89337-0
PIBN 10905695

This book is a reproduction of an important historical work. Forgotten Books uses
state-of-the-art technology to digitally reconstruct the work, preserving the original format
whilst repairing imperfections present in the aged copy. In rare cases, an imperfection in
the original, such as a blemish or missing page, may be replicated in our edition. We do,
however, repair the vast majority of imperfections successfully; any imperfections that
remain are intentionally left to preserve the state of such historical works.

CATALOGUE

OF THE

COLLECTIONS

OF

Ancient Greek and Roman,

European and United States Coins

OF

FRANCIS LEPERE, M. L. COLEMAN

JEREMIAH ZIMMERMAN, Dr. W. E. BOOKER,

AND

CHARLES S. WILCOX

Splendid set of Gold Dollars.   Round and Octagon, $50.

BALDWIN & CO., $5.

Extremely Rare Canadian Coins, and one of the Finest Collections

of United States Fractional Paper Currency ever offered.

═══════════

CATALOGUED BY

S. H. & H. CHAPMAN

1348 PINE STREET

And to be sold at Auction by

DAVIS & HARVEY, Auctioneers

1112 Walnut Street, Philadelphia

MONDAY AND TUESDAY, FEBRUARY 15 AND 16, 1904

Commencing each day at 2 P. M.

PREFACE.

On careful perusal of the following pages we believe every collector will find some article to interest *him,* and we hope he will make a bid for it, The varied character of the several collections enabling him to do so. We would call attention to the collection of Roman and Greek coins, the complete set of gold dollars, and among which are exceedingly rare mint marks as 1854 San Francisco, 1859 Dahlonega, 1860 Dahlonega, of which probably about 5 in all are known. The California Baldwin & Co. $5, one of the great rarities, the superb $50 round and octagon. The Wilcox collection of U. S. Fractional Paper Currency is one of the finest yet offered—rivalled only by the great collection of Monroe J. Friedman, which we sold last year; collectors in this series will find about all the notes they lack, and as many of them are the only specimens obtainable should excite keen competition. Canadian collectors will have a chance to enrich their cabinets with the finest Owen Ropery, side view pennies and half pennies, rare proofs, unique Carrit and Alport, Bridge Tokens, etc.

No lot is separated—all described under each lot number are sold under that number, at so much each piece, no matter how many there may be in it, except where *set* or *lot* is stated.

Owing to several persons sending in bids and not paying for the goods bought and delivered to them, it has become necessary to request collectors unknown to us to send bank reference with their bids or to pay in advance for the lots purchased for them. We find our practice of examining each bid letter on receipt, and instructing the bidder where he appears uninformed as to values, or is probably making a mistake in the lot number, gives much satisfaction to our numerous clients. All letters received four days prior to the day of sale receive this examination. Many errors are thus corrected, often considerable sums saved to the bidder—and also collectors who make bids far below current market value when so informed concentrate the sum they desire to spend on lots within their means, thus securing more than they otherwise would.

Priced catalogues will be supplied after sale on receipt of 75c. (stamps taken, any denomination). Payment required with order.

We charge 10 per cent. additional to the price the lot is knocked down for on those purchased by us for our bidders, as our commission for executing the bids, purchasing and shipping. The auctioneers will attend to bids free of this charge, but they assume no risks or responsibility for shipment, and require payment to be made before delivery of the goods.

This has been the rule of the trade for thirty years or more, and we may add that it is an arduous undertaking to enter and attend to the thousands of bids received, the majority of which are unsuccessful and on which there is no remuneration. We have city customers who come to the rooms in person, examine the collection and leave us their bids, paying us the 10 per cent. commission on bills of $300 to $500.

All coins, medals or paper money sold by us are guaranteed genuine, and this holds good indefinitely.

Very respectfully,

S. H. & H. CHAPMAN,

NUMISMATISTS.   1348 Pine Street,

Philadelphia.

SCALE.

4   8   12   16   20   24   28   32   36   40   44   48   52   56   60   64

CATALOGUE

——◆——

COLLECTION

OF

FRANCIS LEPERE, Esq.

PUEBLO, COL. (Formerly of St. Louis)

——◆——

AMERICAN COLONIAL COINS.

1 1652 Massachusetts pine tree shilling. Large type. Good. Small piece trimmed off right edge for ¼ of an inch.

2 1652 Massachusetts pine tree shilling. Small type. Fair.

3 1652 Massachusetts oak tree sixpence. The very rare variety with MASATHVSETS only on obv. Very good. Dent in center and hole in right field.

4 1652 Massachusetts oak tree six pence. Obv. worn smooth; trace of a few letters and tree. R. Very good.

5 (1681) New Jersey. Mark Newby half penny. Fair; usual condition.

6 (1681) New Jersey. Mark Newby farthing. Good.

7 (1681) New Jersey. Mark Newby farthings. Var. poor. 3 pcs.

8 1722 Rosa Americana. ½, 1, 2 pence, uncrowned rose *with date.* Complete set. Fair. 3 pcs.

9 1722, 3 Woods ½ p. 1723 far'g (scarce). Fair. 3 pcs.

10 1730 Pa or Bung Town. Geo. II. GEORGE RULES. Gd.

11 1760 Voce Populi. Varieties. Fair. 4 pcs.

12 1766 Pitt token. Bust of Pitt. NO STAMPS. R. Ship AMERICA at bow. Superb example. Light olive. Rare.

13 1767 Louisiana. With R F counterstamped and without. Fair.   2 pcs.

14 1773 Virginia. Geo. III. Bust. R. Arms ½ p. Original bright red.

15 1779 Rhode Is. Map of island, troops, etc. R. Ship; ornament removed from below. Brass. Very good.

16 1785 Vermont. Sun and hills. VERMONTIS. Holed at top, otherwise very good. Rare.

17 1786 Vermont. Sun and hills. VERMONTENSIUM.   9 trees. Very good. Light olive.

18 1787 New York. NOVA EBORAC. Liberty f. r. Planchet cracked to nose. Very good.

19 1789 New York. Mott's clock card. Good.

20 1794 New York. Talbot Allum & Lee Cent. Good.

21 1796 N. Y. Castorland. Beautiful design for $½. Restrike. Bronze proof.

22 1787 New Jersey. Horse head and plow. Large die. Good.

23 1787 New Jersey. Large nosed horse. Over a Conn. cent. Very good.

24 1788 New Jersey. *Small horse* on reverse before legend. Very good.

25 1788 New Jersey. Horse head faces *to left*. Good.

26 1787, 8 Mass. cents. Good.   2 pcs.

27 1787 Mass. half cent. Corroded surface. Very good.

28 (1791) Kentucky. Hand with scroll OUR CAUSE IS JUST. Plain edge. Ex. fine.

29 (1791) Kentucky. As last. Very fine.

30 (1791) Kentucky. As last but *edge lettered*. Good. Nicks.

31 (1791) Kentucky. As last but *edge lettered*. Fine. Scarce.

32 1787 Auctori Plebis. Bust. R. Female seated. Vg.

33 (1791) Bar cent. U. S. A. R. 13 bars. Extremely fine. Very rare.

34 *C* 1781   North American token.   Female seated.   R.   Ship. Good.

35 *C*   Ships, Colonies and Commerce.   U. S. and British flags. Very fine.   2 pcs.

36 *C* 1794   Franklin Press cent.   View of Press.   Very fine.

37 *C* 1787   Franklin or Fugio cent.   Sun dial, MIND YOUR BUSINESS.   Original red color.   Unc.

38 *c* 1776   Continental dollar.   Sun dial CURENCY.   Pewter, all but 1 are so.   Good.

39 *C* 1783   Washington cents.   3 types.   Good.   3 pcs.

40 *C* 1793   Washington.   Bust left.   Same obv. as small eagle cent of 1791.   R.   Ship sailing r.   Very fine.

41 *C* 1795   Washington.   Bust.   R.   LIBERTY AND SECURITY. Fine.

42 *C* 1795   Liberty and Security, as on last.   R.   Hope. IRISH HALF PENNY.   Rare.   Mule.   Very good.

43 *C* 1795   Washington.   Bust r.   R.   Fire grate.   ½ penny. Uncirculated.

44 *C*   Male slave kneeling.   AM I NOT A MAN?   Very fine.

45 *C*   Various Colonial and State issues.   Poor (some do not show date).   No Conn.   75 pcs.

46 *C*   Connecticut cents.   Unassorted.   Poor to good.   1 holed. Some do not show date.   60 pcs.

U. S. GOLD COINS.

47 *L* $5 1891   C. C. Mint.   Very fine.

48 *L* $5 1899   S. Mint.   Very fine.

49 *C* $3 1878   Extremely fine.   Mint lustre.

50 *L* $2½ 1850   Fine.

51 *L* $2½ 1861   Very fine.

52 *L* $1 1851   O. Mint.   Light pin scratches on obv.   Vg.

53 *L* $1 1851   Fine.   R.   Has had solder removed from it.

54 *L* $1 1862   Very fine.

55 *L* $1 1862   Very good.

56 *C* $1 1889   Uncirculated.   Last year of issue.

57   Japanese gold dollar.   Very fine.

4 U. S. SILVER DOLLARS.

UNITED STATES SILVER COINS.

DOLLARS.

2 62 58 1795 Head of liberty. Two leaves under each wing. Very good.

2 50 59 1795 Head of liberty. Three leaves under each wing. Very good.

2 25 60 1795 Bust. Very good. Very scarce.

1 40 61 1796 Large date. Poor. 1797, 6 stars facing. Very good. Both holed. 2 pcs.

2 20 62 1797 6 stars before bust. Two file scratches on neck. Very good.

3 90 63 1797 7 stars before bust. R. Small letters as used on 1798 15s. Small eagle. Good. Very rare.

1 90 64 1798 Wide date, 8 touches bust. Fine.

1 50 65 1798 Close date. Fine. Weak in center on stars on rev.

1 50 66 1798, 1799 Poor. 2 pcs.

1 70 67 1799 over 1798 Fine. Stars sharp, even milling.

1 70 68 1799 No berries on laurel. Fine.

1 80 69 1799 Same obv. R. With berries on laurel. Fine.

2 60 70 1799 Fallen 9, erratic date. Very fine. Scarce.

2 15 71 1800 Perfect date. Very good. Bold impression, even milling.

3 72 1802 over 1. Very fine. Scarce.

2 15 73 1803 Small 3. Very good. A lightly pin-scratched on bust.

2 10 74 1803 Large 3. Good. Slight dent on reverse edge.

9 50 75 1836 Very fine. Rare.

1 40 76 1840 Fine. Scarce.

77 1841 Very fine.

78 1842 Very fine.

79 1844 Very fine. Scarce.

1 30 80 1845 Very fine. Scarce.

81 1846 Very fine.

82 1847 Fine.

83 1848 Very fine. Scarce.

84 1850 Extremely fine. Scarce.

(left-margin handwritten annotations shown in italics)

/.6c 85 C 1857   Fine. *...........................*
Cl.K *2.-* 86 C 1859   Proof. *.....................*
Puck */.40* 87 L 1870   Proof. *...........*
4 4 */30* 88 L 1872   Fine. *.........*
.... */.25* 89 C 1873   Standard.   Last year of this type.   Fine. *....................*
..' *.:* 90 L 1877   Trade.   S(minute).   Phil. Mint.   Vf.   2 pcs.
..... */ —* 91 L 1878   Standard.   S. Mint.   Phil. 7 feathers.   C. C. (2).
                               Good.   4 pcs.
.... */.2c* 92 L 1878   Standard.   Carson City Mint.   Ex. fine.   Rare. *..........*
           2.05 93 C 1879   Metric dollar.   Very good. *...............*
Jia */.50* 94 C 1879   Trade dollar.   Brilliant proof. *...............*
...... */.25* 95 L 1879   Standard.   New Orleans Mint.   Fine. *........*
v'. */. —* 96 L 1879   Standard.   New Orleans Mint.   Very good.   3 pcs.
.... */.i0* 97 L 1879   Standard.   San Francisco Mint.   Good.
...... */.15* 98 L 1880   Standard.   New Orleans Mint.   Fine. *..........*
C: *.:* 99 L 1880   Standard.   San Francisco Mint.   Fine.   Rare.
C. *.:* 100 — 1880   Standard.   O. Mint 1.   S. Mint 4.   Vg.   5 pcs.
C) */.-* 101 L 1881   Standard.   San Francisco Mint.   Fine.   Nicked
                               on cheek.
dcre */.15* 102 L 1881   Standard.   New Orleans Mint.   Fine. *..........*
C. */.* 103 L 1881   Standard.   N. O. and S. Mints.   Very good. 2 pcs.
...Bior */.15* 104 L 1882   Standard.   New Orleans Mint.   Uncirculated.
                               Slightest abrasion. *...............*
C. */.30* 105 L 1882   Standard.   Duplicate of last in every respect. *........*
/ Pele */.40* 106 L 1882   Standard.   C. C. O. S. Mints.   Good.   3 pcs. *..........*
Clcu */.10* 107 L 1883   Standard.   Carson City Mint.   Very good. *..........*
l. C. */.10* 108 L 1883   Standard.   C. C. and O. Mints.   Vg.   2 pcs.
• C. */. —* 109 L 1884   Standard.   S. and O. Mints.   Vg.   2 pcs.
C. */.* 110 L 1885   N. O. and S. Mints.   Very good.   2 pcs.
Offur */.10* 111 L 1885   N. O. and S. Mints.   Good.   2 pcs. *..........*
. .11 */15* 112 L 1886, 1887, 1888.   New Orleans Mint.   Vg.   3 pcs. *..........*
'C. */.* 113 L 1888   San Francisco Mint.   Poor.   O good.   1889 O
                               very good.   3 pcs.
Ucoy */.10* 114 L 1890   N. O. Mint.   Very good. *..............*
. C. */.* 115 L 1890   N. O. and S. Mints.   Good and fine.   3 pcs.
/rib. */.25* 116 L 1891   S. O. C. C. Mints.   Good. *..........*   3 pcs. *..........*
/R2 *.:/.10* 117 L 1892   C. C. S. O. Mints.   Good. *110 Rich....D.*   3 pcs. *..........*

115 118 L 1893 C. C. and S Mints. Good. *115 Richard* 2 pcs.

1.30 119 L 1893 New Orleans Mint. Uncirculated. Mint lustre.

1. 120 L 1894 O very fine. S good. 2 pcs.

1.05 121 L 1895 O very fine.

1. 122 L 1895 O very good and fine. 2 pcs.

1.10 123 L 1895 S. Uncirculated. Slightly chafed.

1. 124 C L 1895 S. Uncirculated, very slightly chafed.

1. 125 L 1895 S. Uncirculated, very slightly abraded. 2 pcs

1. 126 L 1896 S. and O. Mints. Fine. 2 pcs.

2.57 127 C 1896 Bryan dollar. Struck by the Gorham Co. to show what would be size of U. S. dollar at the market value of silver. R. Wheel to show size of U. S. 412 grain dollar, whereas this one has 823 grains. Edge dented. Fine.

1. 128 L 1896 O. Mint. Extremely fine, slightly abraded.

1.05 129 L 1896 S. Mint. Good.

1.10 130 L 1897 O. Mint. Very fine.

1.— 131 L 1897 O. Mint. 1898, S. Mint. Vg. 2 pcs.

1.25 132 L 1898 S. Mint. Proof surface. Slight abrasion on cheek.

1.10 133 L 1899 O. Mint. Extremely fine.

1. 134 L 1899 O. and S. Mints. Very good. 2 pcs.

1 135 L 1899 S. and O. Mints. Very good. 2 pcs.

1.25 136 L 1900 N. O. Mint. Uncirculated.

1.10 137 L 1900 N. O. Mint. Uncirculated.

.50 138 L 1900 S. Mint. $1, $½, $¼, $1/10. Uncirculated. Mint lustre. 4 pcs.

1.60 139 C L 1900 Washington and Lafayette, heads r. R. Statue to Lafayette at Paris. Uncirculated.

1.60 140 C L 1900 Washington and Lafayette as last. Very slightly abraded.

1. 141 L 1901 O. (2) and P. Mints. Very good. 3 pcs.

.56 142 L 1901 S. Mint. $1, $½, $¼, $1/10. Unc. Very slight abrasion. 4 pcs.

143 C 1904 Roosevelt Medal. Bust of the President. PRES. THEO. ROOSEVELT. R. View of the beautiful HALL OF FESTIVALS AND CENTRAL CASCADES EXPOSITION ST. LOUIS 1904. Silver. Brilliant proof. Same size and weight as a dollar.

HALF DOLLARS.

4. - 144 1794   Good.   Very rare. *[handwritten]*

24. 145 1794   Good.   Hole at RT has been skillfully filled and *[handwritten]* re-engraved. Shows file marks before bust. *[handwritten]*

80 146 1795   Fair. *[handwritten]*

22. - 147 1796   16 stars. Good. Has had a hole over head filled *[handwritten]* and so skillfully done, the E being re-engraved as to be *[handwritten]* almost invisible. Extremely rare. *[handwritten]*

21. - 148 1797   Fair. Date very strong. Extremely rare. *[handwritten]*

320 149 1801   Good. Very rare. *[handwritten]*

330 150 1802   Good. Very rare. *[handwritten]*

1. - 151 1803   Large date. Good. *[handwritten]*

60 152 1805   5 berries on laurel branch. Good. *[handwritten]*

460 153 1806 over 1800. Die cracked through bust. **Very good.** Extremely rare, as much so as 1796. *[handwritten]*

2.05 154 1806 over 1805 Good. Die cracked before bust. Vr. *[handwritten]*

60 155 1806   Blunt 6, wide date. Very good.

53 156 1806   Blunt 6, close date. 1810, good. *[handwritten]*   2 pcs.

90 157 1807   Bust r. Very fine. *[handwritten]*

90 158 1808   Extremely fine. Scarce. *[handwritten]*

75 159 1809   Very fine. Sharp, even impression. *[handwritten]*

60 160 1809   Good. *[handwritten]*

S.2 161 1810, 1811, 1812. Very fine. *[handwritten]*   3 pcs. *[handwritten]*

130 162 1813   Extremely fine. Strong, even impression. *[handwritten]*

120 163 1814 over 1813. Very fine. *[handwritten]*

70 164 1814   Perfect date. Very fine. *[handwritten]*

4.50 165 1815   Fine. Very rare. *[handwritten]*

3.5 166 1815   Good. Very rare. *[handwritten]*

.85 167 1817 over 1813   Very fine. Scarce. *[handwritten]*

75 168 1817   Open date. Die cracked. Date 1 81 7 with center dot under ear. Very good. *[handwritten]*   2 pcs.

80 169 1818   Large date, over 1817, the 7 showing above 8. Very fine. *[handwritten]*

60 170 1818   Small date over 1817, the 7 blurring 8. Fine.

40 171 1818   Perfect small date. Very fine. *[handwritten]*

85 172 1820 over 1819   Fine. Scarce. *[handwritten]*

173 1820   Perfect date.   Small 2.   Fine.   Scarce.

174 1820   Perfect date.   Large 2.   With and without knob.
Very good.   Scarce.   2 pcs.

175 1821   Extremely fine.   Sharp impression.   Scarce.

176 1821, 1824, 1827, 1832, 1834, 1838.   Good.   6 pcs.

177 1822   Wide and close dates.   Extremely fine.   2 pcs.

178 1823   With center dot on neck.   Uncirculated.

179 1823   Without center dot.   Light scratch in field.   Unc.

180 1824 over 1820, 1821, etc.   Very good.   Scarce.

181 1824 over 1821   Uncirculated, slight abrasion on cheek.

182 1824   Double profile.   Very fine.   Sharp stars.

183 1825   Large date, no back to the 2.   Uncirculated.

184 1825   Slightly smaller date, back to 2 on base line.   Ex.f.

185 1826   Wide date.   Ex. fine.   Slight proof surface.

186 1826   Close date.   Uncirculated.

187 1827 over 1826 and large curled 2.   Good.   2 pcs.

188 1827   Flat bottom 2.   Uncirculated.   Mint lustre.

189 1828   Curled 2 with and without knob to 2.   Square based
2 with small and *large* 8's.   Very good.   4 pcs.

190 1829   Recut or over date 9.   Very fine.

191 1829   Perfect date.   Uncirculated.   Mint lustre.   Slight
abrasion

192 1830   Small O.   Uncirculated.

193 1830   Large O.   Extremely fine.

194 1831, 1832, 1833.   Uncirculated.   Lustre.   3 pcs.

195 1832   Large letters on rev.   Very good.   Scarce.

196 1834   Large and small dates.   Ex. fine.   2 pcs.

197 1834   Large date.   R. Large letters.   Unc.   Scarce.

198 1835   Semi *proof* surface.   Extremely fine.

199 1836   Semi proof surface.   Uncirculated.

200 1836   *Milled edge.*   50 CENTS on rev.   Very fine.   Rare.

201 1837   Uncirculated   Mint lustre.

202 1838   Uncirculated.   Very slightly abraded.

203 1839   Uncirculated.   Very slightly abraded.

204 1839   Liberty seated.   Drapery from point of elbow.
Ex. fine.

205 1840, 1842 large date O.   1848 O, 1849 O. and P.   Very
good.   5 pcs.

206 1842 Large and *small* date, latter rare. Vg. 2 pcs.

207 1843, 1844 Very fine. 2 pcs.

208 1845, 1847 Very good. Scarce. 2 pcs.

209 1846 Tall and small 6. Fine. 2 pcs.

210 1849 Extremely fine. Mint lustre.

211 1850, 1851 Good. 2 pcs.

212 1851 New Orleans Mint. Fine.

213 1851 Duplicate. Good.

214 1852 Very fine. Rare.

215 1852 New Orleans Mint. Fine. Rare.

216 1853 Arrowheads at each side of date. R. Rays behind eagle. Unc. Mint lustre. Only year of this type!

217 1856, 1858 O. (2), 1859, 1860 O. S small; 1861, 1862 S small; 1866 S no motto (poor). Good. 8 pcs.

218 1860 *Plain edge.* Struck to one side. O. Mint. Very good. Unique.

219 1875 C. C. S. 1877 rev. engraved with initials. 1877 S. 2 positions of S. Good. 5 pcs.

220 1892 O. S. P. Mints. 1893 S., 1894 S., 1895 S., 1897 S. O. 1898 S. (2). Very good. 6 pcs.

221 1892, 1893 (5). Columbian. Ex. fine and Unc. 6 pcs.

222 1893 Columbian. Uncirculated.

223 1898, 1899 O. P., 1900 O. P. S., 1901 P. (2), O., 1902 O. (2), 1903 O. Very good to uncirculated. 12 pcs.

QUARTER DOLLARS.

224 1796 Fair. Rare. 1st year of denomination.

225 1804 Fair. Rare. 2d year of denomination.

226 1805 '6 over 5 and perfect date. '7, '15, '18 (3), '19 (2), '20, '21 (2), '22, '25. Poor to good. 15 pcs.

227 1824 Good. Rare.

228 1828 Extremely fine.

229 1831, '33, '34, '36, '38 (2 types), '39, '43, '44, '45, '46, '48, '49, '50. Fair to good. 14 pcs.

230 1832, 1835, 1837. Very fine. 3 pcs.

231 1840 no drapery from elbow, '41, '42, '44, '47, '51, '54, '56, '57. O. Mint. Good.   11 pcs.

232 1852, '3, '4, '5, '7, '8, '63, '5, '6, '7, '70, '1, '2. Very good.   20 pcs.

233 1853 Without arrow head at sides of date. No rays behind eagle on rev. Good. Very rare.

234 1855 (poor, scratched), '64, '65, '67, '69, '74, '75, '76, '77, '88, '91, '92, '93, '95, '98, 1900. *San Francisco Mint.* Good.   18 pcs.

235 1867 Brilliant proof. Rare.

236 1873 without and with arrow heads, '4, '6, '8, '9, '80, '3, '5, '91, '2, '6, '7, '9, 1900, '1. Good to fine. 17 pcs.

237 1875 Carson City and San Francisco Mints. Unc.   2 pcs.

238 1876 C. C. high, very fine; C. C. low, good; '7, good; '8 Unc. *C. C. Mint.*   4 pcs.

239 1879, '81, '2, '6, '7, '9 (2), '90, '1. Unc.   9 pcs.

240 1891, '2, '3, '4, '5, '6, '7, '8, 1900, '1, '2 (3). Good to Unc. *New Orleans Mint.*   14 pcs.

241 1893 Columbian. Head Queen Isabella of Spain. Unc.

DIMES.

242 1796, 1805, 1807, 1809, 1811, 1822. Poor.   6 pcs.

243 1811 holed; 1814, '20, '1, '3, '7, '9, '30, '2 to '39. Poor.   22 pcs.

244 1824 over 1822. Very good. Scarce.

245 1829, '31, '2, '3, '4, '5, '6, '7 (both types), '8, '9 (O. Mint), '41, '2, '3, '5. Fine and very fine.   18 pcs.

246 1841 to 1857 incl., '59 to '62, '68, '70 to '76 (struck off center), '78 to '87, '89 to '92, '94, '96 to '99. Includes 1846 (flattened out), 1853 no arrow heads, 1856 large date, 1873 both types. Good to unc. (few of latter since 1879). Diff.   51 pcs.

247 1840, '1, '54, '6, '7, '8, '91 to '94, '6, '8, '9, 1901, '2. All O. Mint. 1860 stars, '4 to '7, '9, '73 arrows, '75 (S. inside wreath, Ex. fine), '88, '90 to '93, '5, '7, '8. All

S. Mint.   1875, '6, '7·   All C. C. Mint.   Diff.   Fair
to unc (a few).   35 pcs.

/0 248 L· Duplicates of last two lots.   Poor to unc.   29 pcs.

./0 249 L·1846   Very good.   Scarce.

HALF DIMES.

/50 250 L·1794   Fair.   Rare.

77· 251 L·1795   Fine.   Surface corroded.   1800 fine.   Plugged
over head.   2 pcs.

7 252 L·1829 to 1873.   P. O. S. Mints.   No rare dates.   Poor to
fine.   Diff.   45 pcs.

5· 253 l· Duplicates from last lot.   Poor to good.   39 pcs.

.35 254 C 1842   Uncirculated.   Mint lustre.   Scarce.

45 255 L·1846   Fair.   Dented.   Rare.

75 256 C 1860   O. Mint.   Uncirculated.   Mint lustre.

8 257 L·1851   O. Mint.   1853, 1855.   3c.   Fine.   3 pcs.

CENTS, HALF CENTS, MINOR COINAGE.
CENTS.

4.15 258 L·1793   Chain.   AЛERICA.   Fair.   Very rare.

/.60 259 C·1793   Wreath.   Fair.   Dent on edge.

2. – 260 C 1793   Liberty cap.   Cracked die.   Obv. poor.   Date
shows.   R. Good.   Very rare.

.50 261 L·1794   Hays No. 33.   Good.

50 262 l·1795   Lettered edge.   Good.   Surface deeply corroded.

28 263 C 1795   Plain edge.   1796.   Liberty Cap and Bust.   Fair.
3 pcs.

2. – 264 C·1799   Date fair, rest of cent very poor.

25 265 L·1800   Dot in first O, break in die.   Good.

25 266 L·1801, '2 no ends, and ends to stems.   1807 over 6.   1808.
1810.   Good.   6 pcs.

25 267 L·1803   Small $\frac{1}{100}$.   Very fine.   Slight dark spot before
and behind head.   Light olive.

4.75 268 L·1804   Perfect date.   Surface corroded all over.   Good.
Very rare.

1.5 269 L·1808   Good.   Steel color.

5½ 270 L·1809   Poor.   Date shows well.   Rare.

271 1811 over 1810 and perfect date. Fair. 2 pcs.

272 1816 perfect die. 1817 knobbed head, wide and close date. Fine. 4 pcs.

273 1820 perfect die. 1827. 1828 over date, 1830 inner line. 1834 large date, 1835 3 var., 1836 p., and b., dies, 1837 beaded and plain cord. 1838, 1839 4 var. Very good to fine. 17 pcs.

274 1821, 1822, 1823, 1824, 1825. Fair. Varieties. 18 pcs.

275 1857 Large and small dates. Fine. Light olive. 2 pcs.

276 1857 Large and small dates. Very good. 8 pcs.

277 Set of Cents. 1793 to 1857, every date but 1799. 1793 wreath, shows date. 1804 poor, date fair. 1809, 1811 poor. Some var.; 10 dups. Poor to good. 91 pcs.

278 Half Cents. 1804 plain and crossed 4, '6. '7, '9, '25, '6, '8 12 and 13 stars, 1856. Good. 10 pcs.

279 Half Cents. 1825, '6, '8 13 s., '9 (2), '32, '3, '4, '5, '57. Ex. fine. Light olive. 10 pcs.

280 5c. Nickel. 1866-76 incl., 1879, 1881 to 1896, 1901. Very good to very fine. 31 pcs.

281 5c. Nickel. 1866, '8, '9, '70, '2, '3, '5, '6, '8, '80, '3 3 types, '4. 10 proofs, 4 unc. 14 pcs.

282 5c. Nickel. 1866-1901 not consec. 23 1883 no CENTS. Very good to uncirculated. 53 pcs.

283 2c. 1864 to '72 (holed). Good. 3c., 1865, 1879. Cents various dates, some uncirculated. 35 pcs.

284 1c. 1862, '3, '4, '7, '73, '5, '7 (very fine), '8 to '97 incl. Uncirculated. 26 pcs.

285 1c. 1856. Eagle flying left. Copper-nickel. Sharp imp. Proof. Slight dent in center of rev. Very rare and steadily advancing in price.

286 Minor proof set 1883. 1c., 3c., 5c. (3 diff.). 5 pcs., set.

287 Minor proof set. 1889. 1c., 3c., 5c. Last year 3c. piece. Set.

FOREIGN SILVER AND COPPER COINS, ETC.

289 1705 Hungary. Rev. under Rakocsy. Arms. R. Virgin and Christ. ½ Crown. Very fine.

290 Pondicherry. Louis XV. Crown. R. Fleurs de lis. 1 (11), 2 (1), Fanams. Very fine.   12 pcs.

291 1780 Austria. Maria Theresa. Bust of this great woman. Crown. Very fine.

291a 1797, 1808. Bolivia. Potosi mm. Chas. IV. Bust. 1807. Peru. Lima mm. Dollars. Very fine.   3 pcs.

292 1810 France. Medal on marriage of Napoleon and M. Louise. Two flaming torches bound together. Silver. Very fine. Size 18.

293 1811, 1814. Italy. Napoleon. Head. 5 lire. Vg. 2 pcs.

294 1882 Haiti. Head liberty. Dollar. Fine.

295 1883 Hawaii. Kalakaua I. Head. ¼, ½, 1 doll. Very good.   3 pcs.

296 1897 Mexico. Eagle. go. Dollar. Very fine.

297 1899 New Foundland 50c. Canada 5c. (5). Vg. 6 pcs.

298 Japan. Oblong itzbue 2. ¼ itzbue 1. Fine.   3 pcs.

299 Various 20c. size (4), 10c. (2), 5c. or smaller (5 maundy) 22. Very good.   28 pcs.

300 Various base silver 10c. to dol. size. Good.   84 pcs.

301 Various foreign copper coins, 37. Jetons, medalets, 45. Fine.   82 pcs.

302 Ancient Roman. 1st, 2d and 3d br. Quinarius of Augustus. Den. of Geta. Drachm of Corinth (off). Poor to good.   12 pcs.

303 Russia. Peter I. 1689-1725, and others. ¼ (1), 1 (7) Kop. St. Geo. Fine.   18 pcs.

304 Venice. Eagle IMPERO AVSTRICO, 1 3 5 10, 15c. 1852. Very fine.   5 pcs.

305 Argentine, So. Africa, Brazil, Haiti, Porto Rico, etc. Essays or fakes. Proofs. Red.   30 pcs.

306 France. Medalets with prices of provisions during siege 1871. Red. Dif. Size 19.   7 pcs.

307 Victoria and Albert and children, Minute medals, 8, in box like U. S. cent, dated 1851 UNITED STATES MINT DROPS.   Lot.

Very rare. *[handwritten]*

/½ 313*B* Borneo, Liberia, France, England, etc. Unc. Dif. 41 pcs.

2 314*C* Canada 34, Guernsey, Gibraltar, etc. Good to fine. 43 pcs.

3 315 *B* Germany States and Cities. Many old. *Different.*
Good to fine. *[handwritten]* 214 pcs.

3½ 316*B* Italy 22, Low Countries 27, etc. Different. Good to fine.
[handwritten] 111 pcs.

½ 317 Various foreign coppers, mostly German. Poor. 121 pcs.

2½ 318*B* Base silver and nickel. Various. *Different.* Good.
[handwritten] 128 pcs.

4 319*G* Base silver and nickel. Very fine. *Different.* 60 pcs.

1½ 320*B* Base silver. Duplicates. Poor to good. 68 pcs.

321*B* Lithuania. Sigismund. Aug., 1555-66 (11). Bohemia.
Wenzel II, 1300-5 (11). Very small coins. Fair.
22 pcs.

322 Various South American silver coins. $¼, 1/5 size. Poor
to good. 22 pcs.

323*B* Various silver coins. Dime and half dime size. Poor to
good. 69 pcs.

324 Roman bronze coins. 1st B. (4), 2d br. 13, 3d 58. Poor
to good. 75 pcs.

AMERICAN MEDALS.

325 *E* Columbus. Bust l., Indian and Columbia at sides. R.
Beautiful females, cupids, etc. Exquisite medal struck
at Milan. Bronze. Proof. 38.

326 Columbus. Bust in cloak l. R. Germania, globe, ship,
etc. Struck at Nuremberg. Bronze. Perfect. 44.

327 Columbus. Bust in ruff l. R. Columbus landing at San

Salvador. Dies by Lea Ahlborn of Sweden. Bronze.
Proof, slight scratch and specks. 32.

328. Columbus steering a boat; Destiny leading him. R.
Tablet. Bronze. Proof. 40.

329. Columbus. Bust with chart. R. Exp. buildings. Br.
Proof. 32.

330. Columbus. Head encircled by sea and three ships used
by Columbus. Struck by the Com. of 100 citizens of
N. Y. Bronze. Perfect. 36.

331. Columbus. Head r. R. Busts of the Pres. of·U. S. from
Washington to Cleveland. Wm., bronzed. Fine. 34.

332. Columbus. Head of liberty l. R. Landing of Columbus.
Bronze. Proofs. Sizes 18, 23, 32. 3 pcs.

333 C Lincoln, A. Bust r. SALVATOR PATRIAE. R. Blank.
Smallest medal of Lincoln. Size 4. Bronze. Perfect. Rare.

334 Grant. Bust l., by Bovy (1868).· R. I INTEND TO
FIGHT IT OUT, etc. Bronze. Slight specks. Vf. 38.

335. Grant. Bust r. R. Tomb. Bronze. Proof. 22.

336. Lafayette. Bust r. R. THE DEFENDER. Copper. Pr. 30.

337 Lincoln. Bust r. by *Ryden*. ABRAHAM LINCOLN * * *
PRESIDENT * 1861 * 1865. R. The North, a man,
and the South, a young girl, under the U. S. flag.
REUNION. Copper, silver plated. Only one we have
seen. Very fine. 40.

2. - *338*. Spanish-American War, 1898. Handsome bronze badge
with suspender of the N. J. Volunteers in the War.
Over all 32 x 60.

339. Washington. Head, cupids. at sides. Centl., 1876. Br.
Proof. 32.

340 L Roosevelt, Dewey. Pins, badges, St. Louis Fair, 1903.
11 pcs.

341 L Centennial, 1876. Memorial (2 var.). Horticultural
Hall. Black walnut, oblong and round. 63. 48. 3 pcs.

2. - *342* C Masonic. Bust of Washington l. SESQUI-CENTENNIAL OF
WASHINGTON'S INITIATION AS A FREE MASON A. L.
5902, etc. R. Head of Medusa in rays. GRAND

LODGE OF PENNSYLVANIA. VIRTUE SILENTIO AMORE.
Bronze. Perfect. Rare. Size 33.

HARD TIMES TOKENS, 1834-1841.

343 C Jackson, bust r. Fair. Holed. Rare. L 3.

344 L Jackson. Obv. as L No. 4. R. As No. 2, but date of
election is 1829 on this token and not 1828 as L, has
it in his book. Extremely fine. Rare.

345 C Jackson, bust r. laureated. Same as last. Fine. Rare. L 4.

346 C Ship l. FOR THE CONSTITUTION HURRAH. Fine. Very
rare. L 6.

347 H L 8, 12 dent, 18, 19, 20, 32, 33, 34, 36, 37, 46, 48,
51 (2 var.), 55, 58, 59, 62, 64, 76, 84, 97, 98, 100,
110, 115, 120. Good to Ex. fine. Nice lot. 27 pcs.

348 L 8 (6), 19 (4), 20 (2), 32 (2), 33 (2), 37, 46, 48 (2),
51 (2), 55, 58 (4), 59, 62 (2), 64, 97 (2), 98 (2),
110, 120 (2). Poor to very good.   38 pcs.

349 H Bust of Jackson with *broad shoulders*. Vg. Rare. L 10.

350 C Jackson standing with sword defending money bags.
Very fine. L 12.

351 C Seward. Bust l. Fair. Holed. Verplanck. Poor.
L 13, 16. Rare.   2 pcs.

352 C Short ground under Jackass. Good. Ex. rare. L 17.

353 C Tortoise with safe. R. Jackass. Uncirculated. L 20.

354 C Liberty head. R. NOT partly erased. Fair. Rare. L 21.

355 C Liberty head, 1 small star at each side of date. L 22.
L 23 altered on rev. L 29 dented. Vg. Rare. 3 pcs.

356 H Liberty head l. Very good. Scarce. L 28.

357 C Liberty head l. Weak in center as usual. Good. Rare.
L 29.

358 H Liberty head l. Extremely fine. Very rare. L 30.

359 C L 31, 32, 33, 34, 36, 37, 38, 39, 44, 45, 46, 47, 48, 51 (3
var.), 53, 58, 60, 62, 64, 67, 68, 69, 76, 80, 83, 84,
86, 92, 94, 95, 97, 98, 99, 100, 103, 104, 107, 111,
113, 117 dent, 120, 122 dented, 123 124, 132, 148.
Good. Some scarce. Diff.   48 pcs.

360 ¼-L 44, 45, 55. Unc. Number in field in ink. 3 pcs.

361 Jackson in safe. R. Jackass. *Brass.* Vg. Rare. L 52.

362 Big head Jackson in safe. Very fine. Weak on ins. as usual. L 53.

363 Loco Foco. 1838. MINT DROP. Very good. L 55.

364 Van Buren. Bust l. THE SOBER SECOND THOUGHTS OF THE PEOPLE ARE O K. Cop. Holed. Vg. L 56.

365 Van Buren. Same. *Brass.* Very good. Rare. L 56.

366 Liberty. R. MINT DROP. Unc. Scarce pres. L 38.

367 Liberty r. R. SPECIE PAYMENTS SUSPENDED. Good. Rare. L 40.

368 Slave kneeling. AM I NOT A WOMAN? Unc. L 54.

369 Same, very fine.

370 Slave kneeling. AM I NOT A MAN? Uncirculated. Brilliant bright red. Rare preservation.

371 Same. Very fine. Scarce.

372 Same. Very good.

373 Liberty l. 1837. R. Ship. 1841. Leaves instead of stars. Very fine. Rare. L 65.

374 Steer r. *A friend to the Constitution.* Good. Rare. L 66.

375 Hathaway. Providence 1833. Fire grate. Unc. L 74.

376 Benedict & Burnham. Waterbury, Conn., 1837. Very good. Scarce. L 109.

377 Crossman. Head liberty, 1837. Very fine. Rare. L 112.

378 Dayton. Head liberty, 1837. Good. Rare. L 114.

379 Feuchtwanger 3c. arms of N. Y. Very good. L 117.

380 Feuchtwanger 1c. eagle and snake, 1837. Vf. L 120.

381 Feuchtwanger's cents, 1837. Very good. L 120. 5 pcs.

382 Maycock. Eagle, 1837. Uncirculated. L 126.

383 Smith's clocks, 1837. Uncirculated. L 135, 136. 2 pcs.

384 Sweet. Head liberty. 1837. Thick pl. Vf. Rare. L 140.

385 Sweet. As last but thin planchet. Vg. Rare. L 140.

386 Bergen Iron Works store. 1840. Eagle. Stars. Very

70 388 C Bucklins West Troy. Big piece cut from edge, but coin is unusually good. L 145.

40 389 C Riker. N. Y. Very good. L 153.

50 390 ₦ 1837-1857. Satirical medal on hard times. Hog hanging. . NEVER KEEP A PAPER DOLLAR—IN YOUR POCKET TILL TOMORROW, hog with snout in jar marked $10. Copper. Proof.

391 C Same. Brass. Proof. Good pocket piece, as it will not wear down.

2 392 H. Store cards, 12. Politicals, etc., 6. 2 holed. Vg. 18 pcs.

1⁄4 393 L Store cards, 13. Reb. tokens, 20. Politicals, 18. 51 pcs.

394 L Square and compasses, radiant G in center. R. Card of J. J. St. Louis, Greenbay, Wis. Unc. Rare.

15 395 L Kunkel's opera troupe. C. S. on 2 reales, 1773. Rhea souvenir silver plated plaque. 2 pcs.

5 396 WA Rubber store card of Paul Friedman, San Francisco.

4.20 397 T. Atwood's card. Equestrian statue of Washington r., GEORGE WASHINGTON. BALE AND SMITH N. Y. R. CARRY ME TO ATWOOD'S RAILROAD HOTEL 243 BOWERY AND MY FACE IS GOOD FOR 3 CENTS. Uncirculated. Very rare.

WAR OF THE REBELLION, 1861-1865.

NECESSITY MONEY.

U. S. unused postage stamps in brass framed, mica covered case, with advertiser's name on reverse, and which passed current at face value. Fast becoming very rare and being appreciated as a purely necessity medium of exchange during a war. Prices in parenthesis are what they sold for at our auction of the Wilcox collection, November 6-7, 1901.

398 C Ayer's Cathartic Pills. 1c., with arrow heads at side of period. Very fine. ($3.80.)

399 B Ayer's Cathartic Pills. 3c., with arrow heads at side of period. Very fine. ($3.80.)

400 Ayer's Cathartic Pills. 5c. Very fine. Not in the great Wilcox set!

401 Ayer's Sarsaparilla. 1c. Very fine. ($2.50.)

402 Ayer's Sarsaparilla. 3c. Fine. ($3.10.)

403 Bates, Jos. L. 1c., period after BOSTON. Vf. ($3.50.)

404 Burnett's Standard Cooking Extracts (3). Kalliston 1.
The metal frames only, *stamps removed.* 4 pcs.

405 Dougan. New York. 1c. Very fine. From Wilcox
collection. ($6.25.)

406 Drake's Plantation Bitters. S.T. 1860. x. 3c. Very fine.

407 Drake's Plantation Bitters. S.T. 1860. x. 5c. Fine.
Mica blistered. ($4.)

408 Gault. R. PAT AUG 12. 1862. J. GAULT. 10c. Fine.
($2.50.)

409 Hunt & Nash, Irving House, N. Y. 12c. Mica broken,
piece of it out, otherwise fine. Very rare. From
Wilcox sale. ($12.)

410 Kirkpatrick & Gault. 5c. Very fine. ($4.25.)

411 Shillito. Cincinnati. 5c. Cinnamon brown. Mica
broken. Very fine. ($7.50.)

412 Rebellion Tokens passed for Cents. Patriotic devices and
ins. Heads of celebrated men. Adv. of store keepers.
Very good to uncirculated. Different. 100 pcs.

413 Rebellion Tokens. Similar. Cleaned red. 75 pcs.

414 Rebellion Tokens. The two curious and rare errors.
SHOOT HIM ON THE SPOOT. SHALL BY PRESERVED.
Fine. 2 pcs.

COLLECTION
OF
M. L. COLEMAN
MOUNT VERNON, ILL.

FOREIGN SILVER DOLLARS.

415 Abyssinia. Menelick. Bust r. R. Lion. Bril. Rare.

416 Argentine. Sun. R. Arms in wreath. 1815 poor; 1834
fine. 2 pcs.

417 Austria. Ferdinand I. Bust r. no date. Good.

418. Austria. Max. I. Bust. 1616. Spot in field. Fine.

419. Austria. Leopold I. "Hog mouth." Bust. 1695. Fine.

420. Austria. Maria Theresa. Bust. 1780. Ex. fine.

421. Austria. Fr. Jos. I. Head. 2 gulden 1859. Double thaler 1867. Very good: 2 pcs.

422. Austria. Fr. Jos. I. Head. 5 kroners for Austria and Hungary. Very fine.   2 pcs.

423. Baden. Leopold. Head. Crown thaler 1834. Very fine.

424. Bavaria. Max. Jos. 1754. 1816 sword and sceptre on rev. 1818 Cube, MAGNA CHARTA. Max II. Double thaler 1854. Fair. All have head.   4 pcs.

425. Bavaria. Otto. Head. 5 Marks 1888. Good.

426. Belgium. Lion defending liberty 1790. R. Arms around sun. Defective planchet. Good.

427. Bolivia. Bust of Bolivar; 1827. Very fine.

428. Bolivia. Same, 1836; also 1874 with arms. Good. 2 pcs.

429. Brabant. Philip II of Spain. Bust left, with titles of King of Spain and England, etc., 1558. Very good.

430. Hesse-Cassel. Frederick II. Bust. R. Star VIRTUTE ET FIDELITATE. Thaler, 1778. Issued to pay the Hessian troops for fighting against the Americans in the Revolutionary War. Fine. Sold at our sale June 3-4, 1903, lot 1184; for $5.20.

431. Brabant, Albert and Elizabeth; no date. Francis I, 1763. M. Theresa, 1765. Jos. II (head), 1785. Good. 4 pcs.

432. Brazil. 960 reis, 1820 (2). 200 r., 1834. 2000 r., 1865. Fine.   4 pcs.

433. Bulgaria. Alex. Arms. 1884. Very good.

434. Ceylon. Geo. IV. Head. R. Elephant. Rix dollar ($¼ size), 1821. Very fine.

435. Chile Volcano, 1833. Condor, 1876. Condor on rock, 1895. Very good.   3 pcs.

436. China. KIANG NAN PROVINCE. KWANG-TUNG PROVINCE. PEI YANG ARSENAL. All have dragon. Fine. 3 pcs.

437. Cochin China. France seated, 1886. Very fine.

438. Columbia Rep. Indian head, 1820. R. Pomegranate. CUNDINAMARCA. Good.

439. Corea. Dragons. 5 YANG. Very fine.

440. Cuba. Head liberty. Souvenir doll, 1897. Very fine.

441. Denmark. Christian V. Cypher crowned, 1672. Good.

442. Denmark. Christ. VIII. Fred. VII. Heads. 1845.
1854. Good. 2 pcs.

443. Dominica. Head liberty, 1891. Extremely fine.

444. Ecuador. Head Pres. 1844. Struck at Birmingham.
Good.

445. England. Anne. Bust. 1707. Poor.

446. England. Geo. III. Head. Bank of England dollar,
1804. Very good.

447. England. Geo. III. Head. R. St. George. Crown,
1818. Very fine.

448. England. Geo. III. As last. Crown, 1819. Very good.

449. England. Victoria. Bust l. R. St. Geo. Crown, 1893.
Very fine. Light scratches.

450. France. Louis XVI. Bust, 1780. a. . Corroded obv.

451. France. Rep. Angel with tablet. Six livres (1791). Vg.

452. France. Napoleon. Head. 5 fr. AN 13. His celebrated straddle coin as on obverse it bears NAPOLEON
EMPEREUR. Reverse REPUBLIQUE FRANCAISE.. Good.

453. Frankfort. Eagle, 1843. Bust of City, 1861. Double
thalers. Very fine. 2 pcs.

454. Genoa. St. John standing. 1795. Good.

455. Germany. Wm. Head. 5 marks, 1874. Very good.

456. Greece. Geo. I. Head. R. Arms. 1876. Good.

457. Guatemala. Carrera, 1864. Liberty seated, 1873. Head
liberty, 1882. Peru doll. c. s. with ½ real die of
Guatemala on obv. and rev., 1894. Vg. 4 pcs.

458. Haiti. Head of Liberty. R. Trophy, 1895. Very fine.

459. Hamburg. Arms. 5 marks, 1891. Very fine.

460. Hawaii. Kalakaua I. Head. 1883. Very good.

461. Hesse. William. Bust. 1771. Good.

462. Hesse. William II. Arms. Thaler. 1832. Fine.

463. Hesse. Louis II. Head. Crown thaler, 1838. Vf.

464. Holland. Knight standing. 1633, nicked on edge. 1790
good. 2 pcs.

2 - 465. Holland. Louis Napoleon. Head. 1808. Very fine.

466. Holland. Wm. II and III. Good and very fine. 2 pcs.

467. Honduras. Liberty standing with flag, left arm on pedestal. 15 DE SEP. DE 1821 above, stars at side, 1878 below. R. Eagle, scroll above. Slight granulation in planchet near edge. Very fine. First we have seen.

468. Honduras. Liberty with flag, etc. 1882. Good.

469. Hong Kong. Britannia standing. 1898. Very fine.

470. Hungary. Chas VI. Bust. 1737. Very good.

471. Ireland. Geo. III. Bank token. Six shillings. 1804. Fine.

472. Italy. Umberto I. Head. 1879. Fine.

473. Japan. Old type and trade doll. Very fine. 2 pcs.

474. Lubec. Arms. R. Eagle. 1752. Very good.

475. Lucca. St. Martin dividing his cloak with a beggar. 1750. Good.

476. Mexico. Ferd. VI. Pillar dollar. 1757. Very fine.

477. Mexico. Chas. III. 1783. C. S. with bust of Geo. III in octagon depression, so as to make it current in England. Good.

478. Mexico. Dolls., 1788, 1804, 1805, 1807, 1810. Good. 5 pcs.

479. Mexico. Zacatecas Provisional doll., 1811. Mountain with cross on apex. L. V. O. Only parts of ins. show as is usual.

480. Mexico. Iturbide. Large and small head. 1822. Fine. 2 pcs.

481. Mexico. Eagle dolls., 1824 hooked neck; 1864, 1867 (Maximilian), 1874, 1872, 1900. Fine. 6 pcs.

482. Milan. Maria Theresa. Bust. 1779. Very good. Scarce.

483. Milan. City standing. Provisional Gov. 1848. Very fine.

484. Naples. Charles, Vesuvius and river god, 1748. Republic, 1799. Liberty standing. Good. 2 pcs.

485. Nassau. Adolph. Head. Double thaler. 1860. Very

486. New Guatemala. Sun and mountains. 1824. Very fine.

487. New Guatemala. As last but dated 1846. Fine.

488. New Guinea. Bird of Paradise. 5 marks, 1894. Brilliant proof.

489. Norway. Christian V. Cypher crowned. R. Arms. 1686. Fine.

490. Norway. Oscar, 1851. Chas. XV, 1862, 1864, 1869. All larger than a doll. Very good. 4 pcs.

491. Nuremberg. Jos. II. Eagle. R. View of City. 1768. Very good.

492. Parma. Marie Louise, wife of Napoleon. Bust. 1815. Very good.

493. Papal. Pius VII. Arms. R. Church on clouds. 1818. Very fine.

494. Papal. Gregory XVI. Bust. 1845. Fine.

495. Papal. See vacant. 1846. Arms. R. Dove in clouds. Very fine.

496. Peru. Ferd. VII. Lima mint mark, 1809. Curious head. Fine.

497. Peru. 1835, 1837, 1883. North Peru, 1838. Good. 4 pcs.

498. Philippine Islands, Porto Rico. Alfonso XIII. Head. 1897, 1895. Fine. 2 pcs.

499. Porto Rico. Alfonso XIII. Head, 1895. Fine. 4 pcs.

500. Poland. Sigismund III. Bust in armor. 1629. Vg.

501. Poland. Alex. I. Eagle. 10 Zlot, 1835. Very good.

502. Prussia. Frederick the Great Thalers, 1751, 1785. F. W. IV thaler, 1860. Good. Poor. Very fine. 3 pcs.

503. Prussia. William I. Head. R. Germania seated. Peace thaler, 1871. Brilliant proof; *very* slight abrasion. Rare condition.

504. Roumania. Charles I. Head. R. Arms. 1883. Vf.

505. Russia. Peter the Great. Bust. Piece cut off top. Scratch.

506. Russia. Alex. II. Head of Nicholas I. R. Equestrian statue erected in honor of Nicholas by Alex. Rouble, 1859. Proof.

507. Salvador. Hand holding flag. 1892. Bust of Columbus. 1895. Very good. 2 pcs.

508. San Marino. Arms. 1898. R. Saint. Ex. fine. Rare.

509. Saxony. John Casimer and John Ernest. Busts vis a vis. 1606. Very good.

510. Saxony. Fred. Aug. 1808. Anton V 1832. F. Aug. 1854. Thalers. John V double thaler 1859. Very good.   4 pcs.

511. Sardinia. Chas. Felix 1828. Chas. Albert 1833, 1844. Good.   3 pcs.

512. Schleswig Holstein. Christ. VII. Head. 1790. Good.

513. Scotland. William and Mary. Busts l. 40 shillings. (½ cr.) 1692. Fine.

514. Siam. Maha Mongkut. Elephant. R. Pagodas. Unc.

515. Sierra Leone Co. Prowling lion. 1791. Vf. Rare.

516. South Africa Rep. Kruger. Bust. 5 shillings, 1892. Very fine. Rare.

517. South Africa. Rep. Kruger. Bust. 3 pence and copper penny, 1892. Unc.   2 pcs.

518. Spain. Dollars, 1762, 1810; Jos. Napoleon, 1818, 1850, 1859, 1870, 1888. Good.   7 pcs.

519. Stolberg. Chas. Louis and Christ. Fred. Stag. 2/3 crown, 1793. Good.

520. Sub Alpine Gaul. Peace and Liberty standing. 1799. Good.

521. Sweden. Gustavus IV Adolph. Bust. R. Solder marks. 1805. Good.

522. Switzerland. Helvetia seated. 1850. Fine.

523. Switzerland. Shooting Fest 5 francs of Basel, 1879. Lugano, 1883. Zurich, 1859. Fine.   3 pcs.

524. Switzerland. Berne. Warrior standing. 1798. R. Arms in oval. Very fine.

525. Switzerland. Geneva. Arms. R. XII FLORINS IX SOLS in rays. 1795. Good.

526. Switzerland. Zurich. Arms and lion. 1622. Fair. Rare.

527. Turkey. Various. Excellent lot. Very good.   pcs.

528. Tuscany. Peter Leopold. 1770. Leopold II. 1856. Sicily. 1753. Good.   3 pcs.

529. Two Sicilies. Murat. Head. 1813. Field polished. Vf.

530· U. S. Colombia. Head liberty. 1869. MEDELLIN. Good.

531· Venezuela. Head Bolivar. R. Arms. Fine.

532· Venice. Lion standing. Edge bruised. Very good.

533· Wurtemberg. William. Head. R. Arms. Double gulden. 1854. Fine.

534· Switzerland. St. Gall. Benedictine Abbey. Bear walking r. 1780. R. Arms. Very good

535 Various countries. 1686, 1692, 1705, 1715, others since 1800. 2 francs (3) and $½ size. Good. 12 pcs.

536 Various. 20c. size, mostly since 1800. Average good. 23 pcs.

537 Various. Dime size (23) includes Alexander the Great drachm. ½ dime size (9). Good. 32 pcs.

538 Rome. Cassius Family. B. C. 342. Head of liberty. R. Temple of Vesta. Denarius. •Very fine.

NUMISMATIC BOOKS, AUTOGRAPHS, NEWS-PAPERS.

539. Montagu. The Copper, Tin and Bronze Coinage and Patterns for Coins of England from Elizabeth to Victoria. 2d Ed. Cuts, 150 p., 8vo., cloth. New.
London, 1893.

540. Scott's Catalogue of Silver and Gold Coins. 27th Ed., 8vo., paper; cover soiled and marked; text clean.
N. Y., 1893.

541. Snowden. Ancient and modern coins in the Mint Coll. 412 pages. 26 embossed plates in colors. 8vo., cloth. Presentation copy with author's autograph.
Philadelphia, 1860

542 Smith, A. M. Encyclopædia of gold and silver coins of the World. Cuts of 6000 coins. 8vo. Cloth. New. Rare. Phila., 1886.

542a Skinner's Standard Money Manual. Cuts of U. S. Coins. 16mo., cloth.   Boston, n. d.

543. Priced Catalogues of Auction sales of Coins, 1900-1 (7). 31 unpriced. 3 $100 Confed. notes.   Lot.

544 Dickeson. American Numismatical Manual. American,

Colonial, State and U. S. Coins. 19 plates, colored.
250 pages. 4to., cloth (faded).   Phila., 1859.

// 545 Newspapers. Pennsylvania Packet, Aug. 3, 5, 7, 12, 14,
17, 21; Sept. 2, also extra., 4, 7, 9, 10 extra., 11, 16,
18, 21, 23. 25, 28, 30. Postscript, Dec. 16, all of
1779. Very fine consecutive set.   22 pcs.

46 546 Dunlap's American Daily Advertiser, July 27, 1793.
Address of citizens of Trenton, N. J., to Washington
and his reply. Phila. Gazette, 15 May, 1801. Poul-
son's Am. Daily Adv., May 15, 1802. Message of
Madison. The Portfolio, Nov. 6, 1802. The Providence Gazette, Oct. 31, 1807; Jan. 13, 1810. N. E.
Palladium, Jan. 17, 1809, in mourning for the Em-
bargo on vessels. Daily Nat. Int., Washington, March
7, 1862. Message of Pres. Lincoln. English papers
of 1746, 1766, 1791. Fine.   11 pcs.

55 546a Confederate States Almanac 1863; Clarke's. Bust of Jeff
Davis. 8vo. Vicksburg.

55 546b Confederate States Almanac 1864. 8vo. Mobile.

60 547 Autographs. Parchment documents signed by Presidents
Jas. Monroe, 1821; John Q. Adams, 1828; Andrew
Jackson, 1831 (badly stained); M. Van Buren, 1839;
Zachary Taylor, 1850.   5 pcs.

.50 548 Pres. McKinley. Card with autograph "Yours very truly
W. McKinley."

25 549 Pres. Roosevelt. L. S. 1900.

250 550 Various authors, actors, governors, mayors, etc., etc. Some
cuttings. About 100.   Lot.

25 551 Washington, J. H., 1813: John, 1792. L. W. and G. C.
and H. D. S. A. L. S.   5 pcs.

/. 552 McKean, Thos., Sig. Dec. of Indep. Chief Justice Pa.,
Gov. Pa., Prest. of Delaware. D. S. 1771. Stained.

/. 553 Monroe, Jas., Pres. U. S. Doc. Sig. Also signed John
Quincy Adams as Sec'y of State, 1822.

/. 554 Johnson, Andrew, Pres. U. S. D. S. Also signed by
Hugh McCullough, Sec'y-Treas., 1865.

/. 555 Calhoun, 1857. Breckinridge, 1859. Vice-Pres. U. S.
A. L. S.   2 pcs.

556 Davis, Jeff., Pres. Confed. States, 1858. L. S.

557 Longfellow, Henry W· Also of his daughter Alice.
A. L. S.   2 pcs.

558 Willis, N. P. Poet, critic and journalist. A. L. S. 4to.
Owego, 1837

559 Lee, Rob. E. A. L. S. 3. pages; also postscript signed.
4to· Slight damage. Dec. 24 (1832).

560 Memminger, C. G. Sec.-Treas. Confed. States. A. L. S.
Official· 4to. Slightly stained.   Richmond, 1862.

561 Confederate Gen's.   J. E. Johnston, J. L. Kemper, A.
R. Lawton, W. H. F. Lee. A. L. S. 8vo.   5 pcs.

562 Ryan, Archbishop of Phila. 8vo. A. L. S. Kenrick,
Archbishop of St. Louis. Sig. Portrait.   3 pcs.

563 Pius IX, Pope. A. Sig., dated 1851. Portrait.   Lot.

564 Rush, Benj. Sig. of Decl. of ·Indep. Fine. A. L. S.
4to., 2 p.   London, 1838.

565 Morris, Robt. Sig. of Decl. of Indep. and Const. A. L.
S. 4to. 1794.

566 Dallas, G. M., Vice-Pres. U. S. A. L. S. 4to. 1847
and 1859.   2 pcs.

567 Cass, Lewis, Gen. A. L. S. 8vo., 2 p. 1857. Cuttings.
Lot.

568 Bancroft, Geo., Secy. Navy and Historian. A. L. S.
L. S. 4to. 1845.   2 pcs.

569 Humboldt, Baron von. Illust. German savant and tra\-
eller. A. L. S. 8vo.   3 pcs.

570 Clay, Henry, Secy. of State, etc. A. L. S. 4to. 1834.
Franked. Portrait.   Lot.

571 Choate, Rufus, Dist. Advocate and Senator, etc. A L. S.
8vo. 1855.

572 Actors. John Holland, 3d person; Effie Germon, Henry
Hall, W. J. Hammond, W. F. Judan, W. H. Hall.
Play bill. 1830. J. H. Wood. A. L. S.   8 pcs.

573 Members of Senate and Congress, etc. Fine lot of A.
L. S.   46 pcs.

INDIAN STONE, SPEAR AND ARROW HEADS.

574 Spear heads. Fine and perfect. Length 6¼ in.

575 Spear. Broad, no shank. Fine. Chip off lower corner, so at time of making. Length, 6 in.

576 Spear. Beautiful shape, shank. Perfect. Very fine. Length, 3 in.

577 Spear. 3 fine 3½ in. long. Arrows 1 to 2½ in. Fine. 36 pcs.

578 Spear and arrow heads. Delaware. 1 to 3 in. Perfect. 50 pcs.

579 Arrow heads. Extreme tip off, otherwise fine, 1 to 2 in. 21 pcs.

580 Arrow heads. White quartz. Perfect. 1 to 2 in. 25 pcs.

581 Wampum. Base silver Maltese cross and amulet of pearl shell, found in Indian grave near Wilmington, Del. 3 pcs.

COLLECTION

OF

W. E. BOOKER, M. D.

WORCESTER, MASS.

CENTS.

582 B.1793 Wreath. Good.

583 C.1794 Hays No. 17. Fine. Badly scratched behind head.

584 B.1794 Hays No. 50. Very good.

585 B.1795 Thin planchet. 1796 Liberty cap. 1806. Poor. 3 pcs.

586 B.1797 Close date; die broken in field behind head. Vg.

587 B.1798 Small close date. Fine. Brown color.

588 B.1799 over 1798. Very good. Cost $20. Ex. rare.

589 B.1800 Perfect date. 1801 perfect 1/100. 1803 small 1/100. Good. 3 pcs.

590 1802 Die broken and chip off edge of rev. Very fine.

591 1804 Broken die. Good. Very rare.

592 1805 Pointed 1. Good. Light nicks. Scarce.

2.— 593 *B*.1807 "Comet Variety." Fine. Steel color.

I. 594 *B*.1808 13 stars. Very good. Bold impression. Steel color.

1.60 595 *g*.1809 Good. Rare.

.18 596 *B*.1810, 1812 large date, 1813, 1814 crossed 4. Vg. 4 pcs.

.80 597 *r*.1811 Perfect date. Good. Nick on edge of reverse.

25 598 *r*.1816 Perfect die. Very fine. Weak imp. Dark olive.

.33 599 *b*.1817, 1818, 1820. Unc. Some original red. 3 pcs.

1.25 600 *b*.1819 Small perfect date. Unc. Pale steel color.

35 601 *C* 1820 Uncirculated. Cracked die. Mostly original red.

1.10 602 *P*.1821 Close date. Very good. Steel color. Slight nicks
              on obv.

9 603 *B*.1822, 1823 over 22, 1824, 1825, 1828, 1829, 1830, 1832,
       1838, 1839 head of 1838. Good. 10 pcs.

1.40 604 B.1826 Close date. Inner line. Ex. fine. Light olive.

.60 605 B.1827 Very fine. Bronzed.

1.05 606 B.1831 Small letters on rev. Very fine. Light olive.

1.30 607 B.1833 Small letters on rev. Very fine. Light olive.

.80 608 B.1834 Small date, connected stars. Vf. Light olive.

2 609 *B*.1835 Small date. Fine. Brown color.

50 610 B.1836 Perfect date. Very fine. Light olive

50 611 *b*.1837 Plain hair cord. R. Large letters. Very fine.
              Light olive.

I 612 B.1840   1, 2, 3, 4 (cleaned), 5, 6, 7, 8, 9. Fine and very
              fine.   10 pcs.

2I 613 B.1850 to 1857. Uncirculated. Bright red, original color,
              slightly smeared but a choice set.   8 pcs.

18 614 B.1835, 1857 ½ cents. Uncirculated.   2 pcs.

COLLECTION

OF THE

Rev. JEREMIAH ZIMMMERMAN

R. Owl. Tetradrachm executed in archaic design for commercial use. Very fine. *l./l:...*

.70 623 ·Same more carelessly struck, only eye and part of head on. Very fine.

1.25 624 ·Dyrrachium. B. C. 250. Cow, calf. R. Pattern. Dr. Very fine. *l:...*

2.50 625 ·Corinth. B. C. 350. Pegasos, exquisitely executed r. R. Head of Pallas l (double-struck). Didr. Vf.

2.60 626 ·Leucas. B. C. 350. Pegasos l. R. Pallas l. Vf. Didr.

2.10 627 ·Leucas. Same. Caduceus behind head. Didr. Vf.

5.50 628 ·Pergamos. *Ionia.* B. C. 200. Cist of Dionysos surrounded by ivy-wreath. R. *ΠEP* Serpents entwined. Tetradr. Very fine.

.55 629 ·Ariarthes VI. *Cappadocia.* B. C. 125-111. Head r. R. Pallas. Drachm. Very good.

.50 630 ·Vardanes I. *Parthia.* A. D. 41-5. Also later Sassanian. Drachm. Fine. 3 pcs.

1.50 631 Volagases IV. *Parthia.* Bust l. R. King seated to whom Tyche offers wreath. Date ℩ϸ = 504 = A. D. 192-3. Fine for this rude tetradr.

.6 632 Sassanidae. Bust of King. R. Altar. Large drachm. Very fine.

.14 633 ·Copper. Various. Poor to good. 25 pcs.

ROMAN COINS.

634 · Republic. B. C. 250. Head of Janus. R. Quadriga. Didr. Very good.

635- Head of Mercury . . R. Prow, ROMA . . Sextans of heaviest struck weight. Fine. Green patina.

636 · Same. Very good. Green patina. As, Cestia. Lowest reduction. F. 2 pcs.

637 · Marcia. Head of King Ancus Martius. R. Statue on bridge. Commemorates the early king and the building of Marcian aqueduct. Den. Fine.

638 · Republic. B. C. 200-50. Interesting types by different moneyers and including specimens struck by Julins Cæsar, Brutus, Sulla. Fine to very fine and worth from 50 cents to $1 each. Denarii. 24 pcs.

IMPERIAL.

639 ⁄ Julius Cæsar. B. C. 45. CAESAR DICT PERPETVO. Head r., laur. and veiled. (Two test marks in field.) R. P. SEPVLLIVS MACER Venus standing. Den. Fine.

640 ·⁄ Same. CAESAR IM Head r. laur. R. Same. Vg.

641 Same. Head of Venus. R. CAESAR Aeneas carrying Anchises and Palladium. Commemorates Julius' claim of descent from Aeneas. Den. Very fine.

642 Same. CAESAR Elephant. Rev. Implements. Fine.

643 ⁄ Augustus. B. C. 28 to A. D. 14. CAESAR AVGVSTVS Head r. R. SIGNIS RECEPTIS, S-P-Q-R. Shield bet. ensigns. Den. ·Ex. fine.

644 ⁄ Augustus and Julius Cæsar. Heads back to back. R. COL-NEM Crocodile chained to palm-tree. 2 Æ. Fine.

645 ⁄ Augustus. OB CIVIS SERVAT(OS). Oak within laurel-wreath. R. S C First sestertius in bronze. Vg.

646 · Augustus. DIVVS AVGVSTVS, S-C. Head l. R. CONSENSV

648 · Same. Fine.

649 · Same. Fine.   3 pcs.

650 · Same. Head l. laur. R. S. C. etc. Caduceus. 2 B. Vf.

651 · Same. Triumphal quadriga r. R. S C TI CAESAR etc.
     1 B. Very good.

652 · Drusus and Tiberius. DRVSVS CAES AVG COS II P(IT)
     Head l. R. TI CAES AVG IM TRP XXXV. Head of
     Tiberius laur. r. Den. Fine. Extremely rare. C. I.
     who states that these were probably struck at Cæsarea
     ten years after the death of Drusus in his honor on
     the late discovery of the crime of Sejanus.

653 · Caligula. A. D. 37-41. Head l. R. VESTA. 2 B. Fine.

654 · Caligula. Head l. R. S. P. Q. R., etc., in oak-wreath.
     1 R. Good.

655 · Germanicus. Head l. R. S. C., C. CAESAR etc. 2 B.
     Fine.

656 · Caligula. S C. Cap. 4 B. Nero. Head. R. CER
     QUINQ ROM. CON Table. Domitian. Bust of Ceres.
     R. Sheaf. 4 B. Fine.   3 pcs.

657 · Claudius. A. D. 41-54. Head r. laur. R. Hope walk-
     ing l. 1 B. Good.

658 · Same. Same rev. SPES AVGVSTA. 1 B. Very fine.

659 · Agrippina Sr. Bust r. R. S C TICLAVD etc. 1 B. Good.

660 · Nero. A. D. 54-68. Head r. laur. R. ROMA seated.
     1 B. Very. good.

661 · Nero. R. Victory flying l. S C. 2 B. Fine.

662 · Galba. A. D. 68. Head r. R. SPQR OB CS in wreath.
     Den. Good.

663 · Galba. Head r. laur. R. LIBERTAS PVBLICA Liberty
     standing. 1 B. Very good.

664 · Otho. A. D. 68. IAP A OTHO (CAESAR) AVGTRP. Head
     r. R. VICTORIA (OT)HONIS Victory flying r. Den.
     Fine. Historical rev.

665 · Vitellius. A. D. 68-9. Head r. laur. R. LIBERTAS
     RESTITVTA(!) Liberty standing. Den. Very good.

666 · Vespasian. A. D. 69 to 79. Head r, laur. R. IVDAEA.
     Judea seated r. before trophy. Den. Good.

during the III consulship (which date this coin bears on the obv.) of Vespasian in A. D. 71 by the Romans under the command of Titus. *~~~~* /25 ~~~~

2.— 668ℓ. Vespasian. Duplicate. Good. C. 239. *~~~~* /0 5 ~~~

3.25 669 Titus as Cæsar. —cos vi=76 A. D. Head r. laur. R. ɪᴠᴅᴀᴇᴀ ᴄᴀᴘᴛᴀ. Palm tree, to r. Judea seated, to l. 1.2.*~~~* pile of arms. 2 B. Fine. C. 117. *~~~~*

670. Domitian. A. D. 81 to 96. Head r. laur. R. S C,
80 .·ᵘ⁴ Emperor standing before him, Germania kneeling. 1 B. Rare. Good. C. 488. *~~~~*

6o 671. Domitian. Same. R. S C. Minerva walking r. 1 B. Very good. *~~~~*

/25 672 - Domitian. Same. cos xi=A. D. 85. R. S. C. Emperor pours libation on altar before temple of Minerva. 1 B. Good. C. 491. *~~~~*

50 673. Domitian. —cos xvii=A. D. 95. Same. R. ɪᴏᴠɪ ᴠɪᴄ-ᴛᴏʀɪ Jupiter seated to left. 1 B. Vg. C. 316. *~~~*

/20 674. Nerva. A. D. 96 to 98. Head r. laur. R. Fortune. 1 B. Good. Scarce. *~~~~*

75 675. Trajan. A. D. 98 to 117. Head r. laur. R. ᴛʀᴘ ᴄᴏsɪɪ ᴘᴘ Peace seated. · 1 B. Fine. *~~~~*

55 676 - Trajan. Same. R. Abundance seated before altar. 1 B. .6ᵒ V. g. *~~~*

3o 677 · Trajan. Same. R. ᴘᴍᴛʀᴘ ᴄᴏsɪɪɪɪ ᴘᴘ. Victory. Den. Vf.

25 678. Trajan. Similar. R. sᴘǫʀ. ᴏᴘᴛɪᴍᴏ ᴘʀɪɴᴄɪᴘɪ. David seated on shield before trophy. 1 B. V. g.

3.6o 679 ꞏHadrian. A. D. 117 to 138. ʜᴀᴅʀɪᴀɴᴠs ᴀᴠɢ ᴄᴏsɪɪɪ ᴘᴘ
ĩᵛ· Bust r. laur. R. ɢᴇʀᴀᴀɴɪᴀ standing. Den. Ex. f. Rare. c. 804. Var. *~~~~*

75 680 ꞏ Hadrian. Head r. laur. R. ᴄᴏsɪɪɪ. Emperor standing.

50 682 , Marcus Aurelius. 161 to 180. Head r. laur. R. FELI-
CITAS AVG IMP VIIII COS III PP. Felicity standing.
1 B. Fine. Green patina.

50 683 , Same. R. IMP VI COS III. Roma seated l. 1 B. Fine.

50 684 , Same. R. IMP VI ( ). Temple of four columns. 1 B.
Good. Rare.

60 685 , Same. R. DESARM. Trophy. 1 B. Good. Rare

75 686 , Faustina Jr. FAVSTINAE AVG PII AVG FIL. Bust r. of
VENUS. Den. V. fine.

1.— 687 , Same. Same types. 1 B. Fine.

50 688 , Same. FAVSTINA AVGVSTA. Bust r. IVNONI LVCINAE.
Empress with three children. 1 B. V. good.

2.— 689 , Same. Bust draped and diademed. R. LAETITIA. 1 B.
Very fine ob., rev. weak.

2.10 690 , Commodus. A. D. 180 to 196. Head r. laur. R. HER-
CVLI ROMANORVM. Emp. as Hercules places hand on
trophy. 1 B. Fine. Rare.

2.— 691 , Clodius Albinus. D CL SEPTA(L)BIN CAES, Head r. R.
FORTRED COSII. Fortune seated l. 1 B. Fine. Rare.

1.55 692 , Pertinax. Head r. R. Providence. Den. Fair. Rare.

85 693 , Julia Domna. Bust r. of Piety. Den. Ex. f.

1.00 694 , Caracalla. A. D. 211 to 217. Bust r. crowned. R.
SALVS ANTONIAVG. Health standing. Den. V. f.

3.25 695 , Same. Bust r. laur. R. PM TRPXVI COSIII PP. Emperor
armed holds Victory in r. hand, at feet captive. 1 B.
Fine. Light green patina. Com. victory over the
Britons.

2.10 696 , Plautilla. Bust r. R. VENVS VICTRIX. Den. Fine.

1. 697 , Macrinus. A. D. 217. Bust r. laur. R. PONTIF MAX
TRP COS PP. Abundance standing. Den. Fine.

80 698 , Same. R. Same ins. Venus. Den. Very fine. Rare.

2.— 699 , Elagabalus. A. D. 218 to 222. Bust r. laur. R. PM
TRPV COSIIII PP. Emp. sacrificing at altar to the god
El Gabel, from which he received his nickname, and
the type that identifies his coins from those of Caracalla. 1 B. Very good.

35 700 , Julia Maesa. Grandmother. Bust r. IVLIA MAESA AVG.
R. PVDICITIA. Modesty. Den. V. f.

V. f.

Same. Fine. Light green patina.

Maximus Cæsar. Bust r. R. PRINC IVVENTVTIS. Cæsar standing with two ensigns. 1 B. Fine. Scarce.

Balbinus. A. D. 238. Bust r. R. PM TRP COSII PP. Peace standing. 1 B. V. g. Cracked.

Pupienus. Bust r. laur. R. CONCORDIA AVGG. Concord seated. 1 B. Fine. Scarce.

Gordianus III. A. D. 238 to 243. Bust r. laur. R. CONCORDIA MILIT. Concord seated l. Large 1 B. Fine.

Philip Sr. 244 to 249. Bust r. of SAECV LARES AVGG. Wolf suckles the twins. 1 B. Very good.

Philip. R. MILIARIVM SAECVLVM. Column on which cos. 1 B. Fine. Com. his celebration of the 1000th anniversary of the foundation of Rome, A. D. 248. Rare. C. 95.

Philip Jr. M IVL PHILLIPPVS CAES. Bust r. R. PRINCIPI IVVENTVTIS. Cæsar standing. 1 B. Fine. Scarce.

Otacilla. Bust r. R. Concord. 1 B. Fine.

Trajanus Decius. 249 to 251. Bust r. laur. R. S C. Mars standing. 3 B. C. 102. Ex. fine. Rare.

Volusianus. 251-4. Bust r. of Concord. 1 B. Fine.

Aemilianus. 254. Bust r. crowned. R. Roma. Den. Fine.

Gallienus. 253-268. Bust r. laur. of VIRTVS AVG. Emp. standing. 1 B. V. g. Scarce.

720. Faustina, Sr. and Jr., Commodus, Severus, Alexander, Gordianus, Philip, Hostilianus. 1 B. All good coins, worth from half to one dollar each. 31 pcs.

721 · Augustus to Philip. 1 B. Poor. Many rare and histori-cal reverses, as Taxes of Nerva. 45 pcs.

722 · Augustus to Hostilian, including Diadumenian and Mac-rinus. 2 B. Poor to good. 45 pcs.

723 · Maximianus, Diocletian, Severina, Maxentius. 2 B. V. f. 7 pcs.

724C Various reigns. 2 Bronze. Poor. 45 pcs.

725 · Era of Constantine. 3 B. Poor to fine. 50 pcs.

726 · Honorius. A. D. 395 to 423. Bust r. R. Roma. Den. V. f.

ENGLISH COINS.

727 · William I. The Conqueror. A. D. 1066-1087. Bust facing, PILLEM REX. R. P-A-X in angles of cross.

727a Ea. Penny. V. f. Bust with scptre.

728 · Henry II 1154 to 1189. HENRICVS REX. Head facing. R. WILLEM ON LV + in centre voided cross. Penny. V. f.

729 · Henry III. 1216 to 1272. IIENRICVS REX III. Head facing. R. WILLEM ON ÇANT (Canterbury). Voided cross reaching to edge. Penny. Very fine.

730C Same. Various moneyers. Fine. 3 pcs.

731 · Edward I. 1272 to 1307. Head facing. Penny. Fine.

732 · Edward III. 1327 to 1377. EDWAR DEI GRA REX ANGL. + FRANC. Head crowned facing. R. CIVITAS LON-DON, etc. Cross. Groat. Fine.

733 · Edward III. Same. Fine.

734 · Henry VI. 1422 to 1461. Same designs of Calais. Time of Joan of Arc. Half groat. Fine.

735 · Henry VII. 1485 to 1509. Bust r. crowned. R. POSVI DEV ADIVTOR ET MEV. Shield on voided cross. Groat. V. f.

736 · Henry VIII. 1509 to 1547. Bust r. Same types. Groat. Fine.

737 · Edward VI. 1547 to 1553. Bust facing, at side VI. R. Same type. Sixpence. V. f.

738. Edward VI. Bust r. R. Ornamental shield, MDXLIX. Earliest date on English coins. Shilling. Poor.

739. Mary. 1553 to 8. Bust to l. crowned. R. VERITAS TEMPORIS FILIA. Shield on cross. Groat. V. fine.

740. Elizabeth. 1558 to 1602. Bust l. R. Shield. 1562 Sixpence. Milled. V. g.

741. James I. 1602 to 1625. Bust r. R. Harp. Ireland Sixpence. V. f.

742. Charles I. 1625 to 1649. Bust l. VI. R. Shield. Sixpence. Fine.

743. Commonwealth. 1648 to 1660. THE COMMONWEALTH OF ENGLAND. Shield. R. GOD WITH US. 1658. Shields VI. Sixpence. V. f.

744. Charles II. 1660-84. Bust by Roettier; mm Crown and plumes. R. Four shields, in angles CC, 1671. Shilling. Unc.

745. James II. 1684-8. Bust l. Same types. William and Mary. Busts r. 1693. Shilling. Good. 2 pcs.

746. Anne. 1702-14. Bust l. R. Shields, 1711. Shilling. V. f.

747. George I. 1714-27. Bust r. R. Shields, S S C, 1723. Shilling. Unc.

FOREIGN COINS.

748. Charles II. *France.* CARLVS REX FR Cross in centre. R. METVLLO +, in centre in mon. KAROLVS. Denar. Fine.

749. Frankfort. Bust of City r. R. Eagle, 1862. 2 thaler. Fine.

750. Brunswick. Wildman. 1621. 1688 Mariegros. Fine. 2 pcs.

751. Bremen. 32 schilling 1748. Double struck. Portugal. Maria I 1797. Good. 2 pcs.

752. Columbia. Indian head. R. Pomegranate. CUNDINAMARCA Dollar. 1821. Very good.

753. Hungary. Francis Joseph. 1000th Anniversary. Bust r. R. Conqueror. Kroner, in case.

ANOTHER CONSIGNMENT OF ANCIENT COINS.

754 Populonia. B. C. 400. Head of Gorgon facing **XXX**.
R. blank. Didrachm. Good.

755 Hyria. B. C. 400. Head of Pallas l. (die broken,
causing face to appear as if bearded.) R. Man-
headed bull to r. Didr. Good.

755½ Metapontum. Head with diadem of vine-leaves. R.
Wheat ear META. V. g. Thurium. Poor. Didr. 2 pcs.

756 Velia. B. C. 400. Head of Pallas facing with signature
of artist across helmet in minute letters *KΛEYΔΩPOY*
R. *ΓEΛ(HTΩN)*. Lion devouring ox-head. R. die much
broken. V. g. Rare.

757 Rhegium. B. C. 500. Man drives biga of mules r. exg.
olive leaf. R. RECINON retrograde. Hare r. Tetradr. Fine. Rare.

758 Gela. *Sicilia.* B. C. 500. Quadriga r. R. *ΓEΛAΣ* retrograde. Man-headed bull r. Tetradr. Fine.

759 Leontini. B. C. 480. Quadriga r. R. Lion's head
within four barley corns. Tetradr. V. g.

760 Syracuse. B. C. 480-460. Quadriga r.; exg. serpent. R.
Head of Arethusa r. with hair in chignon coiled four
turns on neck; around four dolphins. Tetradrachm.
Fine.

761 Athens. *Greece.* B. C. 450. Head of Pallas r. R. Owl.
Tetradr. V. g. Has had hoop soldered to edge.

761a Thebes. B. C. 300. Head of Demeter facing. R.
Poseidon. Didr. Good.

762 Aegina. B. C. 600. Tortoise. R. Punch-mark of 6 div.
Didr. Poor.

763 Thasos. B. C. 200. Head of Dionysos. R. Herakles
standing. Tetradrachm. Good.

764 Dyrrachium. B. C. 400. Cow suckles calf. Didr. Good.

765 Istrus. B. C. 300. Two heads. R. Eagle on dolphin.
Didr. G.

766 Sinope. B. C. 300. Head of City l. R. Eagle facing;
ins. off. Didr. V. f.

1.60 767 . Pergamum. B. C. 200. Cist of Diouysos. R. Serpents.
Tetra. G.

, *1.30* 768 ' Seleucus II. *Syria.* Head r. filleted. R. Apollo. Tetradr. G.

2.70 769 ' Darius I. *Persia.* B. C. 525 to 485. King kneeling r.
R. Punch-mark. Siglos or silver daric. Good.

2.5 770. Darius II. B. C. 425 to 405. Same. R. ΣΘ in p. m.
Good. Rare.

3.50 771 ' Euthydemos. *Bactria.* B. C. 220. Head filleted r. R.
Herakles seated. Tetradrachm. Good. Rare.

1.30 772 · Ptolemy II. Ptolemy VII. Heads of I. Tetradr. Good.
2 pcs.

2.60 773 · Augustus. *Roma.* IMP CAESAR. Head r. R. AVGVSTVS
Altar. Tetradr struck for Asia. Good.

\ *1.70* 774 · Clodius Albinus. Head r. R. VIC AVG COSII. Victory r.
Den. Very fine. Rare.

COLLECTION

OF

CHARLES S. WILCOX, Esq.

CHICAGO, ILL.

OF

UNITED STATES FRACTIONAL PAPER CURRENCY

One of the finest collections ever offered for sale.

*All are uncirculated, perfect, and uncreased or folded, un-
less otherwise stated.*

FIRST ISSUE.

August 21, 1862, to May 27, 1863. Postage Currency.
Act of July 27, 1862. Engraved and printed by the National
Bank Note Co. *A. B. N. Co.* in monogram on reverse.

PERFORATED EDGES.

Jac.   *1.20* 775   5c.   Fac simile of 5c. postage stamp with bust of Jefferson.   Orange paper. *15 Salm p 25 John 65 Salm*

Johnson   *.70* 776   5c.   Same. Vertical pair. *51 Aim*   2 pcs.

Hy.   *.70* 777   5c.   Same device. On buff paper. *55 Salm*

Hy.   *.60* 778   10c.   Fac simile of 10c. postage stamp with bust of Washington. Dark green. *65 Salm*

Johnson   *1.10* 779   25c.   Fac simile of 5 5c. stamps. Perforations touch plate on top. *75 Salm*

all.   *2.10* 780   25c.   Same. Bright orange paper and bright brown color. Perforations touch plate at top. Rare shades. *2.00!*

Hy.   *1.40* 781   50c.   Fac simile of 5 10c. stamps. Dark green. *Salm*

Same as last, but cut edges, without the perf. edge.

9 ail   *25* 782   5c.   Pale yellow paper. Shades from light yellow to deep orange. *25 au 1 Salm 25 John 1 Salm 18 John* pcs.

aim   *21* 783   5c.   Light brown. Vertical strip of 3, creased bet. 3 pcs.*21 aim*

C   *16* 784   5c.   Deep orange. Vertical strip of 4. *// au*   4 pcs.*5 they*

C   *20* 785 C 5c.   Brown on yellow paper. Vertical strip. *au*   4 pcs.

Hessler   *21* 786   10c.   Dark and yellow green.   2 pcs.

aim   *46* 787   10c.   Light green. Vertical pair. Creased between. 2 pcs.*51 au*

Hy.   *32* 788 C 10c.   Light green. Vertical block. Creased. R. Slightly soiled.*16 large*   8 pcs.

C   *25* 789 C 10c.   Light green. Vertical strip. Perfect. Uncsd. 4 pcs.

C.   *35* 790   25c.   Three shades, light to very dark (rare).   3 pcs.

Swan   *50* 791 C 25c.   Light brown. Vertical strip. Creased in dividing line. *Sullivan 3 large*   4 pcs.

C.   *65* 792   50c.   Dark and yellow green.   2 pcs.

C   *65* 793   50c.   Light green. Vertical pair.   2 pcs.*65 Salm*

Swan   *1.10* 794 C 50c.   Deep green. Vertical pair. Uncreased. 2 pcs.*75 au*

65 795 C 50c.   Slightly lighter green. Vertical strip. Lightly creased in div. line.   4 pcs.

Printed by the Government, without A. B N Co on reverse. Same design as above. Perforated edges.

*796   5c.   Brown on light yellow. Perforations touch plate on left end. Rare. *75 Salm*

*105*797   10c. Perforations touch plate on left end. Very fine. *(illegible)*

*165*798   25c. Light brown. Perforations cut off right end into frame. Rare. *(illegible)*

*65*799   25c. Red brown. Perforations cut off upper 1/3 of right end and 1/3 of bottom. Rare. *(illegible)*

150 800   25c. Medium brown; buff paper. Perfection. V. rare. *(illegible)*

*225*801   25c. Yellow brown, pale yellow paper. Perfection. Very rare. *(illegible)*

3.- 802   50c. Light yellow green. Very rare. *(illegible)*

Same as last but cut edges; without perforations.

*75*803   5c. Dark and light brown. One trimmed into frame at top, other at bottom. Very rare.   2 pcs. *(illegible)*

*80*804 c.5c. Light brown on pale yellow paper. Horizontal pair. Slight crease. Very rare. *(illegible)*   2 pcs. *(illegible)*

50 805   10c. Dark green, white paper. Rare. *(illegible)*

65 806   10c. Yellow green. Extremely fine. Rare. *(illegible)*

20 807   25c. Cinnamon brown. Trimmed close all around and into frame on right end. Very rare. *(illegible)*

70 808   25c. Light reddish brown. Extremely fine. Lightly creased. Rare. *(illegible)*

550 809   50c. Bright dark green. Beautiful specimen of this very rare note when in this perfect condition. Cost $7.25. *(illegible)*

SECOND ISSUE.

October 10, 1863, to February 23, 1867, Act of March 3, 1863. Head of Washington in center against background of a scene on a levee, with broad oval gilt band around head. Reverse; large numeral on U. S. shield with open numerals printed on in gold.

Without letters or date on reverse in gold.

15 810   5c. Light and dark brown (3). Slight shades. *(illegible)* 4 pcs. *(illegible)*

17 811   5c. Light brown. ~~Complete~~ sheet of 16. Margin *(illegible)* trimmed close off; into frame at top and left side. *(illegible)*   16 pcs.

*16*812   10c. Slight shades.   2 pcs. *(illegible)*

*35*813   10c. Dark green. Vertical pair. *(illegible)*   2 pcs.

vva~   30 814   10c.   Light green.   Thin 10.   Vertical strip.   Light crease. *Swan 16 Urge.*   4 pcs.

_   25 815   25c.   Violet.   Slight shades.   1 has strip of bottom of obv. offset on it.   3 pcs.

im   1.01 816   25c.   Violet.   Thin, slightly bluish paper. *101 Ain*

Gilt letter and date in corners of reverse.

'   18 819   5c. $ 18 63.   Light brown and darker shade.   One 1863, no letter.   Very fine. *18 Ain*   3 pcs.

C   15 820   5c.   18 63 blurred out.   Pair creased between.   Cut into plate on bottom.   2 pcs.

dee   52 821   5c.   18 63 blurred out.   Deep brown.   Sheet of 20.   Light crease down two rows. *50 ace 18 Urge*   20 pcs.

Jee,   57 822 C   5c.   Cinnamon brown.   18 63 blurred.   Creased in folds. R. Slightly soiled.   Trimmed close at bottom and left end.   Complete sheet. *51 ace 15 Urge*   20 pcs.

By,   32 823 C   5c.   Cinnamon brown.   Date and letter clear. $ 18 63. Vertical strip.   Perfect.   Rare.   3 pcs.

ill   13.~ 824   10c.   1863 blurred out.   *Very thin grey paper.*   Wide even margins.   Only specimen both Dr. Wilcox and ourselves have ever seen.   Cost $15. *W.icec.*

Ulum   26 825   10c. $ 18 63 (clear).   Slight shades. '   3 pcs. *25'*

     25 826   10c. $ 18 63 clear.   Light apple green.   Vert. strip. Perfect.   Scarce.   4 pcs.

     20 827   10c.   18 63 slightly soiled.   No date, perfect.   Vert. pairs.   24 pcs.

dee   57 828   10c.   18 63 blurred out.   Complete sheet of 20.   Faint crease in two rows. *50 ace 16 Urge*   20 pcs.

C   50 829   25c. $ 18 63 clear.   *The 25 S and date in yellow ink ungilt.*   Grey lilac.   Superb block of 4.   Very rare.   4 pcs.

'   35 830   25c. $ 18 63 (clear).   Violet and steel.   Violet (rare).   2 pcs.

'   60 831   25c. $ 18 63 clear and in *yellow, no gold.*   Steel violet. Vert. pair.   Rare.   2 pcs.

C'   30 832   25c.   18 63 blurred date.   No letter.   2 shades.   2 pcs.

     833   25c.   A 18 63   Red violet.   Trimmed to plate on top. R. Not even. '' *Jelle dept | ihe vace | dvd cme*

55 834 25c. **A** 18 63 clear. Shades of deep violet.   2 pcs. *5/...*

8/ 835 50c. **A** 18 63 (blurred). Gilt on rev., narrow and broad.

          Vermillion. *83 Ann.*   2 pcs.

75 836 50c. 1 18 63 clear. Crimson. Perfection.

          Silk fibre. paper which can be split. Gilt letters and date on rev.

40 837 5c. **R** 1 18 63 clear. Trimmed close. Extremely fine. Very rare.

160 838 10c. **T** 1 18 63 clear. Rare. *2.20. 85 Ann.*

146 839 10c. **T** 1 18 63 blurred. Slightly darker shade. Rare. *11 5/Ann.*

210 840 25c. **T** 1 18 63 clear. Deep violet. Margin off on *2.88,* lower and left side into plate. Rare. *20/ Ann.*

150 841 25c. **T** 1 18 63 clear. Light violet. Margin trimmed *75 ..* off upper edge into plate. Gilt ring oxidized. Rare. *160 a...*

1.50 842 25c. **T** 2 18 63 clear. Deep violet. Rare. *1.10 /ale*

211 843 25c. **T** 2 18 63 clear. Pale violet. Rare. *2 // Ann. 2 Ann*

2.- 844 50c. **T** 1 18 63 clear. Deep crimson. Rare. *206 Ann*

.80 845 50c. **T** 1 18 63 clear. R. Gilt; gilt tarnished. Light crimson. Rare.

10 846 ⸦ 50c. **T** 1 18 63 clear. *The back only.* Evidently separated from the face.

2.— 847 50c. **O** 1 18 63. Margin off on lower edge into plate. Very rare. *2. /dRe*

2.- 848 50c. **R** 2 18 63 Perfection. Rare. *2. Ann. /.8 /dRe*

THIRD ISSUE.

December 5, 1864, to August 16, 1869. Act of March 3, 1863.

.5 849 3c. Dark and light curtain or background; portrait also differs. *3./... 30 ... 17 ...*   2 pcs. *...*

40 850 3c. Vertical pairs as last. *... 40 Susan*   4 pcs. *...*

41 851 3c. Vertical triplets as last. *40 Conn. 17 ...*   6 pcs. *...*

40 852 ⸦ 3c. Complete sheet of 25. Creased in folds. Close *16 Ann* margins. Light curtain. Very rare in this shape.

                                             25 pcs.

853 5c. Bust of Clark. With and without plate letter *a*. Green backs.   2 pcs.

854 5c. Bust of Clark. Crimson back. Very scarce.

855 5c. Bust of Clark. Crimson on back. Plate letter *a*. Rare.

856 5c. Bust of Clark. Crimson on back. Complete sheet of 20 notes. The first left hand row has letter *a* showing that there are 4 with *a* to 16 without it. Superb sheet uncreased and believed to be unique as a complete sheet.   20 pcs.

857 10c. Bust of Washington. Plate 1 and without. Green backs.   2 pcs.

858 10c. *Autograph signatures of Colby and Spinner. Carmine back. Rare.*

859 10c. Engraved sigs. Carmine back. Scarce.

860 10c. Engraved sigs. Shading showing on face more than in last. Carmine back. Scarce.

861 10c. Engraved sigs. Plate 1. Carmine back. Rare.

862 10c. *Autograph signature of Jeffries and Spinner.* Carmine back. Very rare.

863 10c. *Autograph signatures of J. Fount Tillman, Register, and Daniel N. Morgan, Treasurer.* Also endorsed by *D. N. Morgan, Treasurer.* Carmine back. Unique. Cost $30. Accompanying this are the autograph cards of both Tillman and Morgan. The 3 pieces sold as 1 lot.

864 25c. Bust of Fessenden. Plate *a* large and small, and no letter. Green backs.   3 pcs.

865 25c. Bust of Fessenden. No plate letters. Carmine back. Rare.

866 25c. Bust of Fessenden. Plate *a*. Carmine back. Very rare.

867 25c. Parchment paper. Plate *a*. Large open gilt work on obv. R. M 2 6 5 in angles. Trimmed to plate on top, into design on rev.

868 25c. Parchment paper. No plate letter. Large open gilt work on obv. R. M 2 6 5 on rev. Has been lightly creased.

869 25c. *Solid small gilt work on obr.* Parchment paper. No plate letter. R. M 2 6 5 in angles. ¼ margin on right end is gone to edge of plate. Splendid example of this exceedingly rare note.

870 25c. Solid small gilt work on obr. Plate *a*. Otherwise as last. Margin off on lower edge and left end on latter into plate. Has been folded but not creased through center. Light green back. Excessively rare. Cost $29.10.

871 25c. *Without any gilt work on obr.* Thin grey paper. Margin off on lower edge. Excessively rare; but two known.

872 25c. Carmine back with *signature of Spinner across back.* Unique.

873 25c. Carmine back with *signature of "Jas. Gilfillan Treasurer U. S."* on back. Unique.

Bust of Francis E. Spinner, Treasurer of U. S., on all to lot 890.

874 50c. Plate 1 *minute.* Plate a. No plate let. R. A 2 6 5. Green backs with 50 in oval at ends. 3 pcs.

875 50c. No let. on back. Greyish and bluish papers. 2 pcs.

876 50c. Plate 1. Bluish paper.

877 50c. Small and large *a*. 2 pcs.

878 50c. Plate 1 *a* (small). Very rare. Slightly plate stained at top.

879 50c. Plate 1 *a* (large). Very rare.

880 50c. Carmine back. R. A 2 6 5. No plate letter. Rare.

881 50c. Carmine back. Plate 1 (minute). R. A 2 6 5. Rare.

882 50c. Carmine back. Plate *a*. R. A 2 6 5. Rare.

883 50c. Carmine back. Plate 1 *a* (minute). R. A 2 6 5. Very rare. Only 1 in a sheet!

884 50c. Same as last. *With autograph of A. W. Wymay Treasurer U S April* 1883 on back. Unique.

885 50c. *Without signatures of either the Register or Treasurer,* the space left for them being blank. R. A 2 6 5. Carmine back. Excessively rare.

886   50c. *Autograph signatures of Colby and Spinner.* R. Not centered and cuts off trifle of right end; does not affect obv. Carmine back. A 2 6 5. Rare.

887   50c. *Autograph signatures of Allison and Spinner.* R. Carmine back. A 2 6 5. Trifle plate stained on obv. margin. Very rare.

888   50c. *Autograph signatures of Allison and New.* R. Carmine back. A 2 6 5. The ink slightly smeared on *Jno* of *News* signature. Exceedingly rare. A. L. S. of Jno. C. New attesting to its genuineness accompanies it. The two sold as 1.

889   50c. *Autograph signatures of Rosecrans and Spinner.* R. Carmine back. A 2 6 5. Exceedingly rare, only 2 ever signed by Rosecrans; the other being in Dr. E. R. Hodge's collection. Cost $56, but likely bring more.

890   50c. Fancy open work back. 50 *Fifty cents* in center. No plate let. Plate 1 small and tall, letter *a* (2) one on bluish paper. Plate 1 *a* small and minute 1. Rare set.   7 pcs.

Justice seated. Reverse as first Spinner 50c. notes.

891   50c. Without plate letter or number; with 1 small and very tall; with *a*. R. Green backs without letters or date.   4 pcs.

892   50c. No plate letter or number. R. A 2 6 5. Green back. Scarce.

893   50c. Large and small 1. R. A 2 6 5. Green back. Rare.   2 pcs.

894   50c. Large *a*. R. A 2 6 5. Green back. Scarce.

895   50c. Large 1, small *a*. R. A 2 6 5. Green back. Very rare; only one to a sheet.

896   50c. Small 1, small *a*. R. A 2 6 5. Green back. Slightly plate stained. Very rare; only 1 to a sheet.

897   50c. Parchment fibre paper; no plate number. R. A 2 6 5. Green back. Trimmed close into plate on right end. Rare.

898   50c. Parchment fibre paper. Plate 1. R. A 2 6 5. Green back. Trimmed close into plate on left end. Very rare.

899   50c. Parchment fibre paper. Plate 1 *a,* large 1 and large *a.* R. A 2 6 5. Green back. Trimmed close on lower edge and right end. Has been creased but hardly distinguishable. Very rare; only 1 to a sheet.

900   50c. Parchment fibre paper. Plate 1 *a,* small 1 and small *a.* R. A 2 6 5. Green back. Plate stained on extreme margin edge on obv. and right end on rev. Very rare; only 1 to a sheet.

901   50c. *Autograph signatures of Colby and Spinner.* R. A 2 6 5. Carmine back. Rare.

902   50c. Autograph signatures of Colby and Spinner. The words *Register* and *Treasurer* omitted. R. A 2 6 5. Carmine back. ~~Possibly unique.~~

903   50c. *Autograph signatures of Colby and Spinner.* R. Without gilt letter or date. Carmine back. Slight plate stain on extreme edge of left end. R. Slightly soiled. Very rare.

904   50c. Parchment fibre paper. *Autograph signature of Colby and Spinner. Register* and *Treasurer* written in. R. S 2 6 4. Carmine back. Slight plate stain on rev. and extreme edge of left end of obv. Very rare.

905   50c. Parchment fibre paper. Engraved signature. R. Carmine back. S 2 6 4. Very rare.

906   50c. Parchment fibre paper. *Autograph signature of Allison and Spinner.* R. S 2 6 5. Carmine back. Water has seriously damaged the signature of John Allison, making it blurred and staining the note around it. Extremely rare.

907   50c. Carmine back. No plate number on obv. R. A 2 6 5. Rare.

908   50c. Carmine back. Plate *a* (small). R. A 2 6 5. Rare. Margin cut close on right end.

909   50c. Carmine back. Plate *a* (large). R. A 2 6 5. Rare. Margin cut close into plate on left end.

910   50c.   Carmine back. Plate 1 (large). R. A 2 6 5. Rare.

911   50c.   Carmine back. Plate 1 *a*. R. A 2 6 5. Slight ink spot on edge of end of rev. Very rare, only 1 in a sheet.

912   50c.   Carmine back. Without plate letters on obv. or rev. Slight plate stain on rev. Rare.

913   50c.   Carmine back. Plate 1 (small). No plate letter or number on rev. Rare.

914   50c.   Carmine back. Plate *a* (small). R. No letter or number. Rare.

FOURTH ISSUE.

July 14, 1869, to Feb. 16, 1875. Act March 3, 1863.

915   10c.   Liberty. Large seal. Minute pink fibre paper. Coarse fibre paper, white, pink, blue ends; last two unwkd. Small seal. Coarse fibre, light blue and slightly darker shade. Allison's name spelled Alleson, Allison and Alleson with dot over e.   6 pcs.

916   15c.   Liberty. Large seal, 2 shades of seal; minute fibre (2), coarse fibre. Wkd.   3 pcs.

917   15c.   Liberty. Large seal. Deep blue end. Coarse fibre. Unwkd. Rare.

918   15c.   Liberty. Small seal. Deep blue end. Coarse fibre. Unwkd.

919   25c.   Washington. Large seal. Minute fibre. Cut close on right end. Wkd.

920   25c.   Washington. Large seal. Violet fibre. Unwkd. Trimmed close on lower edge, into plate on rev.

921   25c.   Washington. Large seal. Deep blue end. Coarse fibre. Unwkd.

922   25c.   Washington. Large seal. Violet blue end. Coarse fibre. Unwkd.

923   25c.   Washington. Small seal. Coarse fibre. Unwkd.

924   50c.   Lincoln. Minute pink fibre. Water marked.

925   50c.   Lincoln. Coarse fibre paper. Water marked.

926   50c.   Lincoln. Coarse fibre paper. Unwkd. Rare.

927   50c.   Stanton. Deep and light blue ends.   2 pcs.

FIFTH ISSUE.

February 26, 1874, to February 15, 1876.

928   10c.   Meredith.   Green seal, long key.   2 shades of seal.
                                  2 pcs.

929   50c.   Dexter.   Light green seal.

930   50c.   Dexter.   Autograph of *Jno. C. New.*   Treas. U. S.
      across face.

SIXTH ISSUE.

931   10c.   Meredith.   Carmine seal.   Long and short key.
                                     2 pcs.

932   25c.   Walker.   Long key (2 shades).   Short key.   3 pcs.

933   50c.   Crawford.

934   50c.   Autograph of *Jno. C. New,* Treas U. S. across back.

935   50c.   Autograph of *Jno. C. New,* Treas U. S. across face.

936   50c.   Autograph of W. S. Rosecrans, Treas. U. S. across
      back.

PROOFS, TRIALS, ESSAYS, ETC.

All of extreme rarity and almost impossible to duplicate any
of them. Many are believed to be unique. The most extensive
collection ever offered.

SECOND ISSUE.

937   5c.   No gilt ring.   Thick buff paper.   Blank rev.
      Trimmed to plate on right end.

938   5c.   As last.   Pair, upper one $\frac{1}{3}$ torn off.   Sold as 1.

939   5c.   As last but thick yellow paper.

940   5c.   As last but thin yellow paper.   Pair, lower one $\frac{1}{2}$
      torn off.   Sold as 1.

941   5c.   As last.   Top line of ins. cut off.

942   5c.   Reverse only.   No gilt work.   Plain paper.   Cin-
      namon brown.

943   10c.   Without gilt ring.   Printed across in 7 lines of
      heavy ornamental type is *First* | *Washington, D. C.* |
      First | *Washington, D. C.* | *Second Baltimore, Md.* |
      Second. | Reverse blank.   Plain paper.   Cost $25.
      Complete vertical sheet—columns of 5.   Wide margins.
                                     10 pcs.

944 10c. As last. Horizontal pair, on one *Second* reversed.
2 pcs.

945 10c. Obv. fully printed. R. Blank, silk fibre paper— one thickness only. Horizontal pair. 2 pcs.

946 10c. Reverse only, apple green, no gilt work. Heavy fibre paper. Vertical strip of two and one-third of another. Trimmed close on left side into plate. Creased in fold. Sold as 2 pcs.

947 10c. As regular issue, without gilt ring. R. Blank. Stiff, heavy fibre paper.

948 10c. Gilt ring only. R. Fully printed, ℧ 1 18 63 in angles. Silk fibre paper.

949 10c. Obv. as issued but band around head is in the ground color (now turned black) and ungilt. R. Without printing but has several directions in pencil for printing. Silk fibre paper that can be separated. small piece off corner; just touching frame.

950 10c. Gilt ring. R. 10 ℧ 1 18 63. No plate printing, only the gilt work as on a regular note. Silk fibre paper.

951 25c. As regular issue *without gilt ring*. On *obverse* is printed 25 (as on reverse usually) and below it in gilt FEBRUARY 20, 1863. R. Violet as regular issue, but shield in blank except for double row of outlined stars. Thin paper.

952 25c. Obv. only, no gilt. R. Blank. Fibre paper. One of the strip cut off the only sheet known (which sold in Friedman Coll. Lot 996, June 3-4, 1903).

953 25c. Obv. only. No gilt. R. Blank. Stiff, coarse paper.

954 25c. Obv. only. No gilt. R. Blank. Stiff plain paper. Vertical pair. Trimmed into plate on left end and slightly rubbed. 2 pcs.

955 25c. Regular obv. on which is Ð 5 18 63 and large 50 as on reverse of regular 50c. note. R. *Green.* As regular issue but the shield blank except two rows of stars outlined across top. Thin fibre paper. Trimmed close on top and right end. Yellow. On back in ink on end *"imperfect proof."* A remarkable oddity.

957   25c. As regular issue with gilt ring. Across upper half heavy printing in gilt of part of a word. R. No plate work only the gilt 25 with 𝕾 18 63 in angles. Plain paper.

958   25c. As regular issue fully printed. R. No plate work, only the 25 in center. Thin plain paper.

959   25c. As regular issue, *no gilt ring*. R. *Blank*. Silk fibre paper, full, as it can be split. "Patent Dry Process."

960   50c. As regular issue but no gilt ring. Obverse only. R. Plank. Heavy fibre paper. Vertical block of 4 and 4. Down the dividing line is written "*Hudsons make of Sept* 11 *Printed* 19, 1863." Cost $20. 8 pcs.

961   50c. As last. Paper slightly thinner. 1 note.

962   50c. As last. Paper heavier than either of above. 1 note.

963   50c. As last. Thin fibre paper. "Patent dry process." (Wilcox.)

964   50c. As last. "Patent dry process." (Wilcox.) Vertical pair. Large margin at bottom.   2 pcs.

965   50c. Reverse only. Deep crimson, no gilt work; other side blank. Fibre paper.

966   50c. As last. Heavier paper. Lighter color. Block of 4 only 1 complete back, the others cut away to $\frac{1}{2}$ (2), $\frac{1}{4}$ (1), another piece consists of portions of 3 notes. The whole sold as 1 lot.

967.   50c. Reverse as regular issue, with the 50c., but on it the gilt ring usually around head of Washington. R. 50 ℟ 2 18 63 in gilt, no other printing. Silk fibre paper.

968   50c. Same. The crimson a trifle lighter shade.

969   50c. The gilt ring only; no other printing. R. The carmine back as regular, but with the gilt 50 ℟ 2 18 63 (blurred) *reversed*. Fibre paper.

970   50c. The gilt ring only; no other printing. R. Fully printed, ℂ 1 18 63. Thin fibre paper.

971   50c. Reverse as regular issue but *without* the gilt 50, etc. R. Shows an elaborate series of designs in lavender. Thick fibre paper.

972 5c., 10c., 25c., 50c. Obv. as regular issue *without gilt ring*. R. The Eagle and border in negative having been punched into plate from a plate or matrix die. 5c. mustard color. 10c. deep green. 25c. deep purple. 50c. pale rose. Numeral of denomination in center in gold and in angles Ð 5 18 63 in gold. Cost $25, and as a set considered by Mr. Wilcox to be unique. 4 pcs.

973 Essay for the 2d issue; design adopted, the denomination left blank. Vignette of Washington inserted in center; beneath the note is the imprint ENGRAVED AND PRINTED AT THE TREASURY DEPARTMENT. On the regular issues this is inside the frame of the notes. No reverse. On plain lemon paper. Broad margin and very interesting and unique proof.

974 50c. G. W. Westbrook's design for a 50c. note. In center fac simile of a $½ of 1863, around EXCHANGE-ABLE FOR UNITED STATES NOTES BY ANY ASSISTANT TREASURER OR DESIGNATED U. S. DEPOSITORY IN SUMS NOT LESS THAN FIVE DOLLARS. RECEIVABLE IN PAY-MENT OF ALL DUES TO THE U. STATES LESS THAN FIVE DOLLARS. ACT APPROVED JULY 17, 1862. 50 in each upper corner; beaded border, scroll corners. R. Fac simile of reverse of $½, POSTAGE CURRENCY FURNISHED ONLY BY THE ASSISTANT TREASURERS AND DESIGNATED DEPOSITORIES OF THE U. S. RECEIVABLE FOR POSTAGE STAMPS AT ANY U. S. POST OFFICE. 50 in each upper corner; beaded border with scroll corners. Engraved by the ruling engine. Black. Printed separately on same piece of thin stiff paper. Creased between the margins. Believed to be unique. Cost $40. We know of the reverse side only which is held at $60.

THIRD ISSUE.

975 5c., 10c., 25c., 50c. Spinner, one with plate *a* white paper. Cardboard proofs. Buff paper. *Faces only.*   5 pcs.

The following have face and back on separate papers. Margins cut to size of note as it would be when issued. Front and back sold as 1 piece.

976   10c.   Autograph signatures of Colby and Spinner. Carmine back.

977   10c.   Autograph signature of Jeffries and Spinner. Carmine back.

978   10c., green back; 25c., both carmine and green backs; 50c. Justice and Spinner, with one green back for the two faces. 5 pieces sold as 1.

979   50c.   Spinner. Autograph signatures of Jeffries and Spinner. Carmine back.

980   50c.   Justice. Autograph signatures of Jeffries and Spinner. Carmine back.

Grant and Sherman 15c. Notes.

All have full wide margins. Face and back printed on separate papers. Face and back sold as 1 piece.

981   15c.   Bust of Grant and Sherman. Engraved sigs. of Colby and Spinner. Vermillion back. Rare.

982   15c.   Busts of Grant and Sherman. Engraved sigs. Green back. Rare.

983   15c.   Busts of Grant and Sherman. *Autograph signatures of Allison and Spinner*. Vermillion back. Very rare.

984   15c.   Busts of Grant and Sherman. *Autograph signatures of Allison and Spinner*. Green back. Very rare.

985   15c.   Busts of Grant and Sherman. *Autograph signatures of Jeffries and Spinner*. Vermillion back. Very rare.

986   15c.   Busts of Grant and Sherman. *Autograph signatures of Jeffries and Spinner*. Green back. V. rare.

987   15c.   Grant and Sherman. *Autograph signatures of Jeffries and Spinner*. Vermillion back. *Cut close—no margin*. Rare.

988   15c.   Grant and Sherman. Eng. sigs. C. and S. Green back. *Cut close—no margin*.

FOURTH ISSUE.

Mong   *130* 989   15c.   Proof on white paper of the reverse only.   Green.

SIXTH ISSUE.

-f   *25* 990   10c.   Proof in black of a design differing from the
adopted one.   Laid down and small piece gone from
corner.'   10., 25c.   Proofs in blue green of adopted
designs.   Backs only.   Small piece from corner and
skelp on 10c.; two corners off on 25c.   From a display
frame prepared by the Columbian Bank Note Co. just
before they failed.   Very rare.   Cost $18.   3 pcs.

fuu. *2.-* 991   50c.   Proof of reverse by Jos. R. Carpenter, Phila.   Horizontal pair—tete-beche.   2 pcs.

The following proofs all have wide margins.   Face and
back printed on separate paper.   Each fully printed
as on issued notes.   Face and back sold as 1 piece.
Second and third issues on paper wkd. C. S. A: SPECI-
MEN in gold on back.

Wim   *26* 992   1st. issue.   5c., 10c., 25c., 50c.   Faces and backs.   8
sold as   4 pcs. *26*

"   *26* 993   2d. issue.   5c., 10c., 25c., 50c.   Faces and backs.   8
sold as   4 pcs.

"   *26* 994   3d. issue.   3c. Washington.   Dark curtain.   Obv. creased
across corner.   Face and back sold as 1.

My   *10* 995   3d. issue.   5c. Clark.   1 face with crimson and green
backs.   3 pieces sold as 1.

Wim   *56* 996   3d. issue.   10c. Washington.   Autograph signatures of
Colby and Spinner.   Carmine back.   Face and back
sold as 1.

L.-   *10* 997   3d. issue.   10c. Obv. has tear ½ inch long—easily re-
paired.   Green back.   Face and back as 1.

A...   *50* 998   3d. issue.   25c. Fessenden.   One face.   Crimson and
green backs.   Three pieces sold as 1.

21 999   3d. issue.   50c. Justice.   *Autograph signatures of Jeffries and Spinner.*   Carmine back.   Very rare.   Two
sold as 1.

/.- 1000   3d. issue. 50c. Justice. Autograph signatures of Colby and Spinner. Green back. Two sold as 1.

/. 1001   3d. issue. 50c. Justice. Eng. sigs. Green back. Two sold as 1.

2.3. 1002   3d. issue. 50c. Spinner. Autograph signatures of Colby and Spinner. Green back—open work. Two sold as 1. *.*

/0.5 1003   3d. issue. 50c. Spinner. Autograph signatures of Allison and Spinner. Crimson back. Very rare. Two sold as 1.

.850 1004   3d. issue. 50c. Spinner. Autograph signatures of Allison and Spinner. Carmine back. Face $\frac{1}{2}$ in. margin. Two sold as 1.

/.- 1005   3d. issue. 50c. Spinner. Eng. sigs. Open work. Green back (has been folded). Two sold as 1.

CONFEDERATE STATES OF AMERICA.

MONTGOMERY, 1861.

Printed by the National Bank Note Co.

4.60 1006 $50 Negroes hoeing cotton. Uncirculated. Brilliant. Very rare. Cost $6.

4.50 1007 $100 Train at station. Very fine. Rare. Cost $9.

3/.- 1008 $500 Train on bridge, man driving cattle to water. Extremely fine, brilliant. Superb example of this great rarity. Cost $56. We know of $60 being paid for one like it.

RICHMOND, 1861.

.3- 1009 $50 Industry and commerce seated. Very fine. Rare. Cost $7.50.

/.- 1010 $100 Train. Extremely fine. Rare. Cost $7.50.

Richmond, July 25, 1861.

7.10 1011 $5 Manouvrier. Letter I. Very fine. The brightest and cleanest specimen we believe we ever sold. Very rare. Cost $9.50.

1012 $10 Female, shield with confederate flag. Heavy paper. Ex. fine.

1013 $20, Ship. $50, Washington. $100, two females. Unc.
         3 pcs.

September 2, 1861.

1014 $5, 4 types; $10, 6 types; $20, 2 types; $50, 2 types; $100. Very fine and uncirculated. 15 pcs.

1015 $5   Group of females. Red and black. Ex. fine.

1016 $10   Group of Indians. Red and black. Ex. fine.

1017 $20   Three females. Green and black. Uncirculated.

1018 $50   Train. Red and black. Unc. Rare. Cost $2.50.

Written dates, 1862.

1019 $100   Negroes hoeing cotton. Train. Unc.   2 pcs.

June 2, 1862.

1020 $1, $2. Uncirculated. Rare in this condition.   2 pcs.

September 2, 1862.

1021 $10   Female on cotton bale. Very fine.

December 2, 1862.

1022 $1, $2, $5, $10, $20, $50, $100. Uncirculated.   7 pcs.

April 6, 1863.

1023   50c., $1, $2, $5, $10, $20, $50, $100. Unc.   8 pcs.

February 17, 1864.

1024   50c., $1, $2, $5, $10, $20, $50, $100, $500. Unc. 9 pcs.

_____

1025   Columbian Exp. Admittance tickets. Six are beautifully engraved portraits of Columbus, Chicago, Washington, Franklin, Lincoln, Handel; others for special days. 3 colored postals.   14 pcs.

1026   Columbian Postal Cards. U. S. 1c. card. R. Beautiful colored views of the Exhibition buildings and surrounding grounds. Series No. 1. Clean. In cover. Different.   10 pcs.

1027   Columbian Postal Cards. As last. 1 extra design; 2 partially written on. In cover.   11 pcs.

1028   Columbian Postal Cards. U. S. 1c. cards. R. Views in black of Exp. buildings. Diff. In cover.   12 pcs.

1029   Album the collection was mounted in. The notes were held in by slits cut in the paper. Clean.

NOTES ISSUED BY THE CONTINENTAL CONGRESS

3/ 1030 C1775 Philadelphia, May 10. $1, $2, $3, $4, $5, $6,
  $7, $8, $30. Good to very fine. *19 Ung*   9 pcs.

3 0 1031C 1775 Philadelphia, Nov. 29. $1, $2, $3, $4, $5, $6,
  $7, $8. Good to very fine. *18 Ung*   8 pcs.

3/ 1032 1776 Philadelphia, Foby. 17. $⅙, $⅓, $½, $⅔, $1, $2,
  $3, $4, $5, $7, $8. Good to unc. *15 Sec 16 ¼ — 8 pcs.*

32 1033C 1776 Philadelphia, May 9. $1, $2, $3, $4, $5, $6,
  $7' $8. Fine. *1 — 4 — 9 Ung: 17*   8 pcs.

30 1034 C1776 Philadelphia, July 22. $2, $3, $4, $5, $6, $7,
  $8, $30. $2 very good; $4 very fine; rest unc. 8 pcs. *18 Ung*

33 1035 C1776 Philadelphia, Nov. 2. $2, $3, $4, $5, $6, $7,
  $8, $30. Fine to uncirculated. *12.*   8 pcs. *21 Ung*

30 1036 C 1777 Baltimore, Feby. 26. $2, $3, $4, $5, $6, $7,
  $8, $30. Very good.   8 pcs. *14 Ung*

37 1037 C 1778 Philadelphia, Sept. 26. $5, $7, $8, $20, $30,
  $40, $50, $60. Very fine and unc. *10 8 pcs.*

215 1038 C 1778 Yorktown, April 11. $4, $5, $6, $7 (torn across,
  mended, good), $10. Fine. Very rare. Lacks $20,
  $30. (Lot worth $25.) *2.0 Ung*   5 pcs.

30 1039 C1779 Philadelphia, Jan. 14. $1, $2, $3, $4, $5, $20,
  $30, $35, $40, $45, $50, $55, $60, $65, $80. Red
  and black notes. Good to unc. Lacks $70.   15 pcs.
  15 Valor.

COLLECTION

OF

C. S. WILCOX, Esq.

UNITED STATES GOLD COINS.

THREE DOLLARS.

4 —1040 C1854 Extremely fine. 1st year of this denomination.

3.90 1041 A1855 Fine. *330*

5.10 1042 C 1856 San Francisco Mint. Very fine. Rare.

6.10 1042a 1857 San Francisco Mint. Very fine. Rare.

1043 ⊂ 1858   Fine. Very rare.

1044 A 1859   Extremely fine. Scarce

1045 ⊂ 1860   Very fine. Scarce.

1046 ⊂ 1861   Very fine. Scarce

1047 1862   Extremely fine. Rare.

1048 ⊻ 1863   Very fine. Very rare.

1049 1864   Extremely fine. Mint lustre. Very rare.

1050 ⊂ 1866   Very fine. Rare.

1051 1867   Very fine. Very rare.

1052 1868   Extremely fine. Faint hair line scratch behind
         head. Mint lustre.

1053 1869   Very fine. Slight abrasion on cheek and field.
         Very rare.

1054 1870   Extremely fine. Rare.

1055 1872   Very fine. Rare.

1056 1873   Brilliant proof. Only 25 made!! Has sold at
         auction for over $100 we believe.

1056a 1874   Uncir. Slight abrasion on obv. Mint lustre.

1057 1878   Uncirculated. Mint lustre.

1058A 1879   Uncirculated. Mint lustre. Rare.

1059BA 1880   Uncirculated. Mint lustre. Rare.

1060 N 1881   Brilliant proof. Rare.

1061 1885   Brilliant proof. Rare.

1062BA 1887   Brilliant proof.

1063 C 1889   Very fine. Last year of issue.

GOLD DOLLARS

1064 1849   Wide wreath. Uncirculated. Semi-proof surface.

1065 1849   Close wreath. Extremely fine.

1066 1849   Dahlonega Mint. Fine. Rare.

1067 1849   New Orleans Mint. Very fine.

1068 1850   Extremely fine. Scarce.

1069 1850   Charlotte Mint. Very fine. Rare.

1070 1850   New Orleans Mint. Very fine. Faint scratch
         on obv. Rare.

1071 1851   Extremely fine. Mint lustre.

1072 1851   Charlotte Mint. Very fine.

1073 1851 Dahlonega Mint. Very fine. Rare. *190 Cm*

1074 1851 New Orleans Mint. Very fine.

1075 1852 Uncirculated. Mint lustre.

1076 1852 Charlotte Mint. Very good.

1077 1852 Dahlonega Mint. Very fine. A scratched below
      head. *250 Usual*

1078 1852 New Orleans Mint. Very good. *250 Usual*

1079 1853 Uncirculated. Mint lustre. A beauty.

1080 1853 Charlotte Mint. Fine. Light scratches on obv.
      Deep dent on edge behind head.

1081 1853 Dahlonega Mint. Fine. Rare. *3 Usual*

1082 1853 New Orleans Mint. Uncirculated. Mint lustre.

1083 1854 Small type. Uncirculated. Mint lustre. Last
      year of type.

1084 1854 San Francisco Mint. Very fine. Ex. rare.

1085 1854 Indian head. 1st year of type. Very fine.

1086 1854 Double outline around head. Only one we have
      seen. Very good.

1087 1855 Uncirculated. Mint lustre.

1088 1855 Charlotte Mint. Very good. Slightly bent.

1089 1855 New Orleans Mint. Very good. Slight dent.

1090 1856 Slanting 5. Very fine. Hair line scratch on obv.

ibly bent.　Minute pin point nick at point of bust.
Excessively rare.　One sold at private sale for $100.
This one has a starting limit of $60. on it.

1105 w 1860　San Francisco Mint.　Very fine.　Very rare.

1106 w 1861　Brilliant proof.　Very rare in this preservation.

1107 w 1862　Brilliant proof.　Very rare in this preservation.

1108 w 1863　Brilliant proof.　Excessively rare.

1109 w 1864　Proof.　Excessively rare.

1110 w 1865　Uncirculated.　Mint lustre.　Extremely rare.

1111 w 1866　Mint lustre.　Very rare in this preservation.

1112 w 1867　Very fine.　Rare.

1113 w 1868　Proof.　Field slightly abraded and edge minute
　　　　nicks.

1114 w 1869　Extremely fine.　Mint lustre.　Rare.

1115 w 1870　Uncirculated.　Mint lustre.　Rare.

1116 w 1871　Uncirculated.　Mint lustre.　Scarce.

1117 w 1872　Uncirculated. . Brilliant. Semi-proof.　Rare.

1118 w 1873　Uncirculated.　Mint lustre.

1119 w 1874　Unc.　Slightest abrasion on cheek.　Mint lustre.

1120 w 1875　Brilliant proof.　Only 420 coined in this year.
　　　　Excessively rare.

1121 w 1876　Uncirculated.　Slightest abrasion on obv.　Rare.

1122 w 1877　Uncirculated.　Brilliant mint lustre.　Rare.

1123 w 1878　Uncirculated.　Slightest abrasion on obv.　Bril'nt.

1124 w 1879　Proof.　Scarce.

1125 w 1880　Unc.　Semi-proof surface.　Mint lustre.　Rare.

1126 w 1881　Brilliant proof.

1127 w 1882　Uncirculated.　Brilliant lustre.

1128 w 1883　Proof.

1129 w 1884　Brilliant proof.

1130 w 1885　Brilliant proof.

1131 w 1886　Uncirculated.　Slightest abrasion on obv.

1132 w 1887　Brilliant proof.

1133 w 1888　Brilliant proof.

1134 w 1889　Brilliant proof.　Last year until St. Louis issue
　　　　1903.

CALIFORNIA GOLD COINS.

1135 1850 $5. Baldwin & Co. Head of Liberty left, diadem inscribed BALDWIN & C, around 13 stars and 1850. R. Eagle with olive branch and three arrows in talons. S M. V (standard mint value) CALIFORNIA GOLD FIVE DOL. Edge milled. Extremely fine. Sharp, even impression. Excessively rare.

1136 1849 $5. Moffat & Co. Type as last. MOFFAT & CO. on diadem. R. Design as last but with periods after each letter of S.M.V. Very fine. Faint scratch before chin.

1137 1851 $50. Augustus Humbert. Eagle on rock, scroll inscribed LIBERTY in beak, above label with 880 THOUS. around UNITED STATES OF AMERICA, below 50 D C. R. Engine turned only. *Edge* AUGUSTUS HUMBERT UNITED STATES ASSAYER OF GOLD CALIFORNIA 1851. Very fine. Sharp impression. Its equal seldom seen.

1138 1855 $50. Wass, Molitor & Co. Head of liberty l., 13 stars and 1855. R. Two branches of laurel enclosing 50 DOLLARS above label inscribed 900 THOUS. Around above SAN FRANCISCO CALIFORNIA, below WASS, MOLITOR & CO. Edge milled. Extremely fine, believed to be second finest known. Very rare. Valued at $350.

75 1144 BA 1881 $½ size. Bust r. J. A. GARFIELD 1881. R. Wreath blank. Round. Very fine.

50 1145 C 1849 Eagle, CALIFORNIA TOKEN. R. U. S flag, cap on staff, steamship above, 1849 beneath, stars at sides 6-7. Size of $20. Brass. Fine. Scratch on obv.

1146 1847 Head of liberty, 13 s. 1847 Below. R. Flag, CALIFORNIA COUNTER. Brass. Size $10. Unc.

1147 C 1849 Head of liberty, 13 s. 1849 below. R. Prospector, CALIFORNIA 1849. Size $5. Some varieties, one is very rare. *Brass.* Vg. to Vf.   29 pcs.

1148 (1849 $2½. Eagle in 13 stars. R. CALIFORNIA MODEL HALF EAGLE 1849. $½ Eagle, 13 stars and 1849. R. CALIFORNIA MODEL HALF DOLLAR. $¼ Eagle, CALIFORNIA 1849. R. MODEL ¼ DOLLAR. Brass. Very fine. The only set we have seen.   3 pcs.

1149 C 1850 Bears waltzing. CALIFORNIA GOLD MINES A D 1850. R. Eagle on sheaf of wheat CALIFORNIA GOLD MINES 1850. Size $20 piece. Milled edge. Copper. Fine. Edge nicked and slightly bent. Rare.

1150 (Carolina. Bechtler dollar. * BECHTLER RUTHERF. (ord -ton) 28G. R. * CAROLINA DOLLAR ONE (sic). Very fine, pin point nick in centre. Slightly bent as usual. Rare.

1151 (Carolina. Bechtler dollar. A. BECHTLER. . * 1 DOL. R. CAROLINA GOLD 27.G 21.C. Very fine.

UNITED STATES SILVER AND COPPER COINS.

1152 V 1857 Dollar. Extremely fine. Semi-proof surface.

1153 1895. Dollar. Brilliant proof. Very rare.

1154 C 1879 ½ dollar. Uncirculated. Mint lustre.

1155 1821 ¼ Dollar. Very fine.

1156 W 1825 ¼ Dollar, Over 1822. Very fine.

1157 V 1828 ¼ Dollar. Very fine.

1158 W 1853 ¼ Dollar. No arrow heads at side of date. R. without rays around eagle. Very fine. Very rare.

1159 1793 Chain and lettered edge. Poor. Dates show.
2 pcs.

1160 1794 Hays Nos. 2, 5, 16, 17, 21, 23, 32, 33, 36, 39, 45
1 undetermined. Poor. Enveloped separately. 12 pcs.

1161 1795 Lettered edge. Slight pits on obv. and edge
dents. Good.

1162 1795 ONE CENT in centre of wreath. Piece off edge.
Fine. Black.

1163 W 1795, 1798, 1803, 10, 14, 16, 17, 18, 19, 22, 24, 25,
26, 27, 28, 29, 30 to 34, 37, 38, 40, 43 to 55, 57.
Poor to good. 38 pcs.

1164 C 1796 Liberty Cap. 6 far from bust. About fine. Black.
Surface lightly corroded.

1165 C 1796 Bust. 6 low. R. Right branch terminates in
twin leaves. Good.

1166 C 1796 Bust. 6 high. R. Right branch terminates in
one leaf, horizontal with opposite leaf. Good. Very
rare.

1167 C 1796 Bust. 6 high; different die to last. Similar rev.
c of CENT far from the E. Good. Very rare.

1168 W 1797 Close date. Die cracked. Good. Dark olive.

1169 C 1798 Very fine. Rich brown color, possibly bronzed
years since. Small date.

1170 C 1800, '01 UNITED, '02 $\frac{1}{000}$. No ends to stems. '03, '05
'06, '07 over 6 and perfect date. Poor. 10 pcs.

1171 C 1804 Perfect die. Very poor. Shows date. Rare.

1172 C 1805 Pointed 1 in date. Very good. Rare.

1173 W 1808 Fine even impression. Olive color. Scarce.
Cost $2.40.

1174 1809 1811 over 10 and perfect date. Poor. 3 pcs.

1175 W 1812 Small date. Very fine. Light olive. Cost $3.40.

1176 W 1812 Small date. Different die from last. Fine.

1177 W 1813 Good.

1178 C 1814 Crossed 4. Fine. Bronze color.

1179 C 1814 Plain 4. Fine. Bronze color.

1180 W 1816 Perfect die. Uncirculated. Sharp stars. Light
olive and red.

1181W 1816   Perfect and broken dies, 1820 perfect die. Very
fine. Dark olive. 3 pcs.

1182 W 1816   Broken die. Uncirculated. Light olive and red.

1183 C 1817   15 stars. Very good.

1184 C 1819 over 1818. Large date. Fine. Brown color.

1185 W 1820   Large 0 in date. Die cracked connecting stars.
Unc. Light olive and red.

1186 C 1821   Very good.

1187 C 1823 over 1822. Good. Scarce.

1188 C 1823   Perfect date. Die badly broken. Restrike.
Fine.

1189 C 1824 over 1822. Wide and close dates. Good. 3 pcs.

1190 C 1825, '26, '27, '28 large and small dates, '29, '30, '31·
Very good. Var.   11 pcs.

1191 W 1832. Large letters on rev. Very fine. Light olive.

1192 C 1833   Extremely fine. Dark steel color.

1193 C 1833, 1834   Double profile. Very good. 1st rare.
2 pcs.

1194 C 1834, 1835   Large and small dates. Very good. 4 pcs.

1195 C 1836   Perfect and broken dies, 1837 beaded hair cord,
1838 very fine. Light olive.   4 pcs.

1196 W 1837   Plain hair cord. Large letters on rev. Unc.
Steel color.

1197 C 1839 over 1836. Good. Rare.

1198 C 1839   Head like 1838. Very fine. Brown color.

1199 W 1839   Silly head. Fine. Dent on edge.

1200 W 1839   Booby head. Very fine. Light olive.

1201 C 1839   Head like 1840. Very fine. Steel color. Scarce.

1202 C 1840   Large date. Very fine. Light olive.

1203 C 1841   Originally a proof. Obv. varnished. R.
Stained. Nick on edge.

1204 C 1842   Large date. Uncirculated. Olive and traces of
original color.

1205 C 1843   Type of 1842. Uncirculated. Faint scratch on
cheek. Light olive.

1206 C 1845   Uncirculated. Steel color.

1207 W 1847   Uncirculated. Brown color.

16 1208 W 1850 (5) 3, 4, 7 ld. Unc. Dark olive.   8 pcs. *1st copy*

5½ 1209 C 1855 Type and size of U. S. cent. R. NOT ONE CENT
         BUT JUST AS GOOD. Very good. Rare.

20 1210 C 1857 Small date. Uncirculated. Light olive and red.

15 1211 C 1857 Large date. Uncirculated. Mostly original red.

HALF CENTS.

1 1212 C 1794, 1795, 1797, 1800, 1802, 1810, 1811. Poor. 7 pcs.

2.05 1213 C 1811 Obv. from original die. R. From die type of
         1803. Restrike. Red. Very rare.

13 1214 W 1803, 4 2 var., 5, 6 2 var., 7, 8, 9, 25, 6, 8 12 and 13
         s., 32, 3, 4, 5, 49 ld., 50, 1, .3, 4, 5, 6, 7. V: g. to
         unc.   25 pcs.

1 1215 W 1803 to 1857. Various dates. Good to very fine. 34 pcs.

20 1216 C 1857 Uncirculated. Red. Last year of denomination.

13 1217 W Hard Times Tokens. Uncirculated. 1 dup.   10 pcs.

CANADIAN COINS.
Arranged according to Breton's book.

75 1218 C 1720 Franco-Americana. Louis XV. Bust r. 1720
         beneath. R. Addorsed L's crowned and forming
         cross; sun in center. Silver. Restrike. Unc. Not
         in Breton.

40 1226 Cṟ 1741   As last. mm. BB. Very good. 508.

1227 Cṟ 1741   As last. mm. V. *Brass.* Date minute. Very fine. 508.

.05 1228 C5 1746   As last. mm. AA. Billon. Fine. 508.

30 1229 C 1751   As last. mm. c. Fine. 508.

.05 1230 C 1751   As last. mm. BB. Brass. Ex. fine. 508.

50 1231 C 1764   As last. mm. A. Billon. Ex. fine. 508.

1232 C 1740   *Half Marque or 12 deniers.* Same type as last. mm. AA. Ex. Fine. Very rare. 509. Last one sold at auction brought $6.50.

1.25   1233 C 1740   Half Marqué. As last. mm. BB. Date weak. Pin scratches on rev. Very good. Very rare. 509.

1234 C 1740   Half Marqué. As last. mm. I. Fine. Very rare. 509.

1235 C 1740   Half Marqué. As last. mm. s. Weak imp., defective planchet. Fair. 509.

2.00 1236 Cn 1740   Half Marqué. As last. mm. T. Fine. Very rare.

1237 Cb 1740   Half Marqué. As last. mm. w. Fair. Very rare.

1238 C5 1740   Half Marqué. As last. mm. x. Good. Very rare.

1239 C 1751   Franco-Americana. Louis XV. Bust r. R. Indian and lilies. Fine. 510.

6.— 1240 T 1754   Franco-America. Bust of Louis XV r. LUD.XV. REX CHRISTIANSS. Uncatalogued obv. The I left out of CHRISTIANISS. No engravers initial on obv.; but on reverse under tree C. N. R. (Roettier?). R. Beavers at work NON INFERIORA METALLIS. Exergue COL. FRANC. DE L'AM 1754. *Silver.* Milled edge. *Original.* Very fine. Very rare and unpublished obv. R. as 514.

1241 C 1755   Franco-Americana. Louis XV. Bust r. R. Galley. Very good. Obv. of 514, reverse of 515.

2.— 1242 C 1815   Magdalen Is. Seal. R. Dried cod. Penny. Very fine. Light brown color; rarely offered so fine. 520.

.5 1243 C 1815   Magdalen Is. As last. Good. Nicked.

1244 C 1837 Habitant. BANQUE DU PEUPLE. *Brilliant proof.*
Extremely rare state of preservation. 521.

1245 C 1838 *Side View Penny.* R. Beaver's tail wide and
points to bottom of ꞵ; ornament on left side points
between AN of BANK. See our Chaloner sale catalogue
plate V No. 2. Uncirculated. Light olive. Superb
example. Excessively rare. 523.

1246 C 1838 *Side View Halfpenny.* To right of building,
fence has 3 bars to left of tree and 5 bars to the right;
to the left of building, fence has 5 bars to right of
tree, and 8 to left of tree. R. Beaver's tail covers
top of left stem of M, rose turned to left. See Chaloner Cat. No. 3, plate V. Uncirculated. Light olive,
slight flakes out of planchet on edge of reverse. Very
rare. 524.

1247 C 1838 *Side View Halfpenny.* To right of building
fence has 4 bars to right of tree and 3 to left. To
left of building fence has 5 bars to right of tree and
6 to left. R. Beaver's tail touches M, the rose faces
upwards and bends slightly to left; period after
SALUS. See Chaloner Cat. No. 4, B, plate V. Fine.
Slight dent on edge. Very rare. 524.

1248 C 1839 *Side View Halfpenny.* To right of building
fence has 4 bars on either side; to left of building
fence to right of tree has 6 bars and to left of tree
9 bars. Eave points at B of BANK. R. Beaver's tail
touches edge of garter. Ends of scroll close on leaf.
Proof. Light olive. Believed to be the finest specimen known. Extremely rare so. See Chaloner No.
3, 524.

1249 C 1839 Halfpenny. Obv. as last. R. Same as reverse
of the next piece. Extremely fine. Very rare. See
Chaloner No. 4.

1250 C 1839 Halfpenny. To right of building fence has 3

1254 C 1811 Canadensis. Bust left; CANADINSIS VEXATOR, all
letters showing well, the tops of TOR not up. R. Female, RENUNILLOS VISCAPE 1811; letters well struck.
The finest and best struck specimen of this rude piece
that has come under our notice. Very rare. 558.

1255 C 1837 Molson. Still, etc. Very fine. Light olive. *Edge*
milled. Rare. 562.

1256 C Owen's Ropery. Ship r. R. R. W. OWEN. MONTREAL
ROPERY. Superb specimen, the finest known. Proof
surface and of beautiful light olive color. Evenly and
perfectly printed. Excessively rare. Starting limit
of $150 on this piece. 564.

1257 C Shaw & Co., Quebec. Very fine. Light olive. 565.

1258 C Devins and Bolton. Montreal, 1867. Uncirculated.
Mostly original red color. Rare. 569.

1259 C Sharpley. R. Montreal. Fine. Rare. 570.

1260 C Gagnon & Co. Quebec. Beaver. Unc. 571.

1261 C Desjardins, Montreal. Bril'nt proof. Bright red. 575.

1262 C Tremblay, Montreal. White metal. Proof. 607.

1263 C Un Sons. 670, 4, 8, 9, 680, 3, 4, 7, 8, 691, 2, 4, 7,
700, 1, 2, 4, 5, 11, 13, 14, 15, 16. Fair to vg. 23 pcs.

1264 C Lesslie & Sons, Toronto and Dundass. Justice. R.
Plow. *Two pence.* Very fine. Free from damages.
Very rare. 717.

1265 C Lesslie & Sons. ½ pennies. Different rev. dies. Very
good. 718. 2 pcs.

1266 C Archor set. $\$\frac{1}{16}$, $\$\frac{1}{8}$, $\$\frac{1}{4}$, $\$\frac{1}{2}$. 1822. Extremely fine. Large piece very rare and is becoming more so the past few years; seldom being offered. 857 to 860.
4 pcs.

1267 C Nova Scotia. $\frac{1}{2}$ p. 1823. Tall head of Geo. IV extending to below P; the nose pointing at upper part of N. Uncirculated. Light olive. Rare. 867.

1268 C Nova Scotia. $\frac{1}{2}$ p. 1823. Small head extending to $\frac{1}{2}$ of P, nose points at lower part of N. Very fine. 867.

1269 c Nova Scotia. $\frac{1}{2}$ p. 1832. Large head. Unc. 867.

1270 C Carritt and Alport. Halifax. The usual type but in this the head is larger, finer workmanship, and differs in the spacing of the inscription—the wreath on head points to first N, etc. R. Differs in many particulars, the flag is large and passes behind the rigging, the pennant from main mast almost touches T, the bowsprit points to center of O. Border serrated. Edge plain. Bronze proof. Believed to be unique. Limit of $50 on this. 881.

1271 C Carritt and Alport. The usual die. The head smaller than last; the wreath points between N N. R. Flag small and clear of rigging, the bow-sprit points between P O. Border beaded. Edge reeded. Uncirculated. Partly original color. 881.

1272 C Starr & Shannon. Indian and dog. R. Ship. Fine.

3ʃ 1279 C New Brunswick. Half cent, 1861. Fine. 908.

1280 C New Brunswick. Regular issue penny and half penny 1843 struck in silver. Brilliant proofs. Excessively rare. Limit of $18 each on this pair. 909, 910. 2 pcs.

6 o 1281 C North West. Hudsons Bay. Arms. 1 Beaver skin. Very fine. 926.

6 o 1282 C North West. Hudsons Bay. Arms. ⅛ Beaver skin. Ex. fine. 929.

5. − 1283 C New Foundland. $2, 1865. Brilliant proof. Very rare. Cost £3.10 in London. 945.

1 2 o 1284 C New Foundland. 5c., 10c., 20c., 1865. Plain edges. Silver. Proofs. Very rare in this preservation. 947, 8, 9.   3 pcs.

3 o 1285 C New Foundland. 1c., 1865. Bright red. Rare preservation. 951.

9 o 1286 C Penny, 1812. Bust of Geo. III. Wreath wide, meeting at top. Very fine. 957.

2 o 1287 C Penny, 1812. As last but edge nicked or dented. Good. 957.

7 o 1288 C Penny, 1812. Bust as last but wreath narrow and open at top. Fine. 957.

5 o 1289 C Penny, 1812. As last. Good. 957.

50 1290 C Penny, 1812. Obv. as last. R. Without date. Very fine. 958.

2 1 1291 C Penny, 1812. As last. Good. 958.

1 10 1292 C Penny, 1812, Bust with laurel wreath of 12 leaves en-

1208 C Penny, 1813. Large &. Uncirculated. 962.

1299 C Penny, 1813. Same variety. Vf. Nick in field. 962.

1300 C Penny, 1813. Small &. Very fine. Pin scratch in field. 762.

1301 C Penny, 1814. Fine. 962.

1302 C Half pennies, 1812. Ex. fine, 1813 fine. 963 pcs.

1303 C Ship, 1813, ½ penny. Very fine. 965, 966 2 pcs.

1304 C Penny, 1838. Bust l., PURE COPPER REFERABLE TO PAPER. Ex. fine. 967.

1305 C Penny, 1838. Same as last. Fine. 967.

1306 C Penny, 1838. Same as last. Very good. 967.

1307 C Wellington half pennies. Very fine. 969, 971, 972, 978 vg., 979, 981, 986, 987. 8 pcs.

1308 C Wellington penny. Extremely fine. Light olive. 970.

1309 C Victoria Nobis Est. Struck over same or 965. Fine. 982.

1310 C Success to trade. Commerce rules the Main. Vg. 983.

1311 C Wellington penny, 1813. Fine. 984.

1312 C Wellington penny, 1813. Good. 984.

1313 C Wellington-Cossack penny. Extremely fine. Light olive. One of the finest specimens we ever catalogued. 985.

1314 C Wellington-Cossack penny. As last. Fine. 985.

1315 C Wellington-Cossack penny. As last. Very good. Slight nicks.

1316 Wellington penny. Bust l., WELLINGTON & ERIN GO BRAUGH 1814. R. Harp E. STEPHENS. DUBLIN. Ex. fine. Nick on the edge.

1317 C Wellington ½ penny in silver. Extremely fine. Very rare. 989.

1318 C Wellington ½ penny. Copper. Uncirculated. 986.

1319 C Wellington ½ penny. Uncirculated. 987.

1320 C Wellington ½ penny. Tall top to head; the inscription small. R. J of July to left of A. Brass. Very fine. Very rare die. 987.

1321 C Wellington ½ penny. Very good. 988.

1322 C Ship, 1814. Very fine. 990.

1323 Eagle, 1813, 1814, 1815. Fine. 994. 3 pcs.

1324 Irishman standing. PURE COPPER PREFERABLE TO PAPER. Ex. fine. 1009.

1325 Ship r. 1812. Very fine. 1004.

1326 Ship r. Very good. Rare. 1005.

1327 Unpublished penny. Female seated, olive branch in right and cornucopia in left; COMMERCE above. R. Wreath enclosing ONE PENNY TOKEN (in 3 lines). Fine. Very rare.

1328 Anticosta Is. Helmeted head l. 1870. R. Wreath with A at point : enclosing ¼. Red. Proof.

1329 Ship r. R. B M C Possibly Birmingham Mining Co., but similar to several Canadian pieces. Good.

1330 Ottawa. Star. A & H ALSCHULER OTTAWA. R. Coat, MANUFACTURERS OF CLOTHING. Very fine. Size 12.

1331 Clifton. Canada west. Indian head 1863 13 stars. R. W. E. TUNIS GENERAL NEWS DEALER DETROIT CLIFTON, C. W. & MILWAUKEE. Milled edge. Unc. Size 12.

1332 Common Canadian coins and tokens. Good. 9 pcs.

PROOFS AND ESSAYS FOR U. . POSTAGE AND INTERNAL REVENUE STAMPS.

The property of Edward M. Schaeffer, M. D., Washington, D. C.

1333 1st issue. Imperforate. In pairs. 1c. Proprietary. Red (1 rubbed), same in deep blue. 2c U. S. Int. Rev. Light blue, pale pink, pale red. 10 pcs.

1334 1st issue. Imp. 1c. Proprietary. Greenish blue. Strip of 4, last one nearly obliterated. 4 pcs.

1335 1st issue. Imp. 2c. U. S. Int. Rev. Pair and strip of of 5. Very poor. Rusted. 7 pcs.

1336 1st issue Imp. 2c. U. S. Int. Rev. Vermillion. Strip of 6, four unsevered, two separate but attached to the four by gummed paper. Across face is written *Butler & Carpenter* (makers, Phila.). 6 pcs.

1337 1st issue. Imp. U. S. Int. Rev. 2c. Pale green, wide margin to left.

1338 1c. Frame for postage stamp of 1857 issue; vignette removed from plate before this was printed. Black on brown safety paper.

1339 3c. Head Washington l. u. s. POSTAGE above, fasces at sides, value beneath, etc. Pale pink. Laid down on paper marked with signature *D. H. Craig.*

1340 3c. American Match Co., Rock Island. Pale orange. Imperforate. Slight crease across. Excessively rare.

1341. 2c. Bust of McCullough r. u. s. INTER. REV. above 2*2 at sides; TWO CENTS beneath. Block of four in deep blue, imperforate. A disc in centre of each stamp so that if once affixed the stamp could not be removed without cancellation. Small hole in centre of one stamp. Original gum. Extremely rare. 4 pcs.

1342 2c. u. s. in rays. TWO CENTS on label above INTER. REV. on label below. Engine turned border. Black on mottled safety paper. *J. M.* in ink written across it. Attached to a piece of paper bearing "From the National Bank Note Company, No. 1 Wall st., N. Y.," and endorsed "This envelope was found among the papers of the Stamp Commission. This stamp and one other of the same kind was pasted on it. The other is sold."

1343 2c. As last. Red brown on yellow safety paper. Unused. Extremely rare.

1344 10c. Head of liberty l., in each corner X. No ins. Sur stamped across face twice INTERNAL REVENUE. Pair in *maroon.* Single in *green.* 3 pcs.

1345 $2. Washington bust l. below UNITED STATES INTER. REV. TWO DOLLARS. Ornamental border. Three different impressions in black, one on buff safety paper. 3 pcs.

1346 $2. Franklin. Bust r. in diamond. u. s. INTERNAL REVENUE above, TWO DOLLARS below. Brown on safety paper. Cracked from top to bottom. Wide margin.

1347 Safety paper. Different. Trial impressions. 2 pcs.

1348 Elaborate designs in various colors of George T. Jones' patent safety paper. American Bk. Note Co., N. Y. 7½x4 inches.